LODGE

P R E S E N T S

Chef John Folse's

CAST IRON
COOKING

AN HISTORICAL COLLECTION
FROM AMERICA'S CULINARY REGIONS

by Chef John Folse, CEC, AAC

ISBN: 0-9625152-5-6
Library of Congress Catalog Card Number: 99-094609

Lodge Manufacturing Company
P.O. Box 380
South Pittsburg, Tennessee 37380
Phone (423) 837-7181
Fax (423) 837-8279
www.lodgemfg.com

Cover Design
SullivanColeMantooth • Chattanooga, Tennessee
Contents and Interior Text Design
Stacy Dean Griffith

Contents

Foreword from Chef John D. Folse

There are certain memories in life, visions of the mind so to speak, that stay with us forever. No matter where we go, or what heights we achieve in life, simple memories keep us in touch with our roots and constantly remind us of a place called home. My home was Cabanocey, a sugar plantation in St. James Parish, less than 30 miles from the landing site of the first Acadians in Louisiana. Although I moved away from this simple beginning many years ago, it was the memories of growing up here among family and farm that called me back to open my Lafitte's Landing Restaurant in 1978.

I really don't know when I first began to think like a cook. I don't know when I came to realize that cooking was more than preparing food here in South Louisiana, but instead a way of life, a social event, a gathering in the kitchen of those we depend upon most. I do remember though the thousands of Sunday dinners, cooked at the hands of my father, uncles, brothers and cousins, all men, at our family camp on Cabanocey. How could I ever forget Uncle Paul Zeringue's jambalaya or River Road crawfish stew slowly simmered in his perfectly-seasoned cast iron pot. Our task in the kitchen was simple back then, we stirred the pots and we washed the pots. No human being was more proud of his cast iron pots and skillets than Uncle Paul. As a very young boy, he taught me valuable lessons in cooking, none more important than how to care for our cast iron pots. He taught me how to respect the tools of the kitchen and that in turn, they would care for us. When Uncle Paul died, I considered myself extremely lucky to have acquired the collection of pots that he had spent his lifetime caring for. I am now the protector of his skillets!

Second only to Uncle Paul, was my grandmother Regina Waguespack Zeringue. Wow, what a cook! We lived in her home for the first seven years of my life, and I will never ever forget the eggplant and River shrimp casseroles, the skillet-fried chicken or her fabulous chicken and andouille gumbo — all meticulously prepared in her cast iron pots. I thought it strange that she never removed her frying skillet from the back burner of her old gas stove, nor would she scrape the thick layer of cooked-on fat from the outside edge of that skillet. I remember her saying over and over again, "You don't have to do a thing to a black iron pot, it just keeps on cooking." Of course, my dad, Royley Folse, was and still is a fabulous cook. After my mother, Therese, died in 1955 with 8 small children in the house, you can bet he passed on those cooking secrets to us so we could in turn prepare meals. No one will ever make a shrimp and okra gumbo, turtle sauce piquante or crawfish stew to compare with his. Even today, he would think of cooking in nothing other than cast iron, and it's from these three very special people in my life that I have become the cast iron "affectionado" that I am. Today, when viewers of my "A Taste of

4

Louisiana" on PBS series inquire about my love of cast iron, the answer is obvious it's tradition in my family. I say proudly and I state loudly, "I only cook in cast iron!"

Imagine how excited I was when approached by Bob Kellermann and his family at Lodge Cast Iron in South Pittsburg, Tennessee, to create a cookbook celebrating 100 years of cast iron cooking. Bob's great grandfather, Joseph Lodge, founded the company in 1896. The Kellermann and Lodge families still run the company today. Few organizations in America can boast that their products are still sought after 100 years. Fewer can claim that those products, many identical to those of a century ago, are in high demand and remain competitive in the market place. Few, if any, can truthfully state that their products are in full use, will last for another 100 years, and with proper care, another 100 and another 100 after. But, Lodge can! I can think of no company in this country that I, as a chef, am happier to be associated with. I'm even more proud to state that long before I met Bob and his family, I was cooking in Lodge pots.

While thumbing through these pages, you'll notice that I've written a section in this book dedicated to Cajun and Creole cooking. I know that you will enjoy my recipes and those of my fellow chefs. Before cooking any of our dishes, I wish to recommend that you read the stories of our regions and how these special recipes have continued to exist and improve over the last 100 years. Naturally, like all good cooks, we have secrets! Ours is cast iron. In every region of the country showcased in this book, cast iron cooking is a way of life. But as a chef, I can tell you that no matter where you lived in the world, as was true for Uncle Paul and my grandmother, cast iron cooking is the perfect method for you too.

Whether you're preparing a hearty beef stew, cooking a seafood gumbo or trying your hand at Southern fried chicken, there's a cast iron pot or skillet just right for the job. My fellow chefs in this book and I work in professional and home kitchens everyday of our life. We understand clearly that the proper cooking utensils are a must if we are to succeed and, more importantly, enjoy our jobs. As you will see in the following pages, we all cook our most famous dishes, those most sought after by the public and the press, in Lodge cast iron and we think that you should too.

Well, enough for the reminiscing, let's start cooking! I sincerely hope that you enjoy this look into America's regional cooking over the past 100 years. We are proud to share our most coveted recipes with you....as long as you promise to prepare them in Lodge cast iron. So, go ahead, choose the right cast iron pot or skillet for the job, prepare the dish with pomp and circumstance, and remember that you have an opportunity here. Just as Joseph Lodge did 100 years ago, you too can cook and care for a cast iron pot and hand it down to the next generation, thereby creating an heirloom for your family.

5

A Celebration of 100 Years of Cast Iron Cooking

*C*ongratulations! You now own a truly unique cookbook! Created for fans of cast iron cookware, old and new, this book is a celebration of the 100th anniversary of Lodge Manufacturing Company.

My great-grandfather, Joseph Lodge, founded Lodge Manufacturing in 1896. Back then, cast iron was about the only way to cook. Today, as we celebrate the 100th birthday of the company, most good chefs still regard cast iron as the best cookware on the market.

Since the days of the earliest settlers, traditional cooking and traditional cookware have been part of the American culture. Of course, different regions of the country were settled by people with different customs and cultures. As a result, seven distinct regional cuisines developed in the United States.

We have selected a premier chef from each of these regions to share some of their favorite recipes that represent the spices, foods and flavors of their particular cuisines. We've even thrown in two additional cooking styles just for fun. Although the Caribbean and Chuckwagon cooking methods aren't considered cooking regions, they do offer some delicious recipes with a style all their own.

Despite their distinctions, the famous dishes in each of these chapters have one thing in common: they are best prepared in cast iron. So no matter where you live, you can bring each of these nine regional delights into your own kitchen and enjoy creating them in your Lodge cast iron cookware as you learn a little from some of the country's best-known and respected chefs.

We hope you enjoy the book, and we encourage you to keep on cooking in cast iron—we are!

Lodge Manufacturing — 100 years and still cooking!

Sincerely,

Bob Kellermann, President

6

Lodge Manufacturing Company:
A Cast Iron Legacy

ith documented roots as far back as the Middle Ages, cast iron is one of the oldest types of cookware in existence, and in the United States, Lodge Manufacturing has a cast iron legacy spanning 100 years.

Joseph Lodge, a native of Pennsylvania, was the superintendent of the Tennessee Coal and Iron Company in South Pittsburg, Tennessee, in 1896. When the company decided to relocate, Lodge opted to make his home in the foothills of the Cumberland Plateau and establish his own foundry.

Lodge's decision to build a foundry in Tennessee was the beginning of a family tradition. Joseph Lodge founded Blacklock Foundry in 1896 and named it for the plant manager at the time, a loyal employee who is credited with much of the company's early success. When that foundry burned in 1909, a new foundry was built in its current location.

The new facility was incorporated as Lodge Manufacturing Company. Today, the company produces an extensive line of cast iron cookware, including skillets, Dutch ovens, chicken fryers, griddles, bakeware and servingware. The company also produces cast iron amenities, including hearth and barbeque grill accessories.

Today, Joseph Lodge's descendants worship in the same church their great-grandfather helped build. And the family business is still a family affair: Another of Lodge's great-grandchildren, Henry Lodge, is the executive vice president and chief operating officer of the company, and all of the members of the board of directors are descendents of Joseph Lodge.

In addition, Lodge Manufacturing is the oldest and one of the largest employers in the county, employing more than 280 residents from the surrounding area who work in the foundry alongside their brothers, sisters, sons and daughters. In fact, some Lodge employees are third- and fourth-generation foundry workers.

"It just keeps getting better!"

7

Cast Iron Cooking:
Not Just a Great Way to Prepare Great Food

Good cooks know you can cook anything better in cast iron, but cast iron's benefits go beyond taste: Cast iron has nutritional and economical qualities every cook should consider.

One of the most important things about cast iron is its durability. Lodge has been in business for 100 years, and it's quite possible that there are skillets out there that have been around as long as the company has.

Cast iron has also proven to be a very economical way to cook. Because cast iron heats evenly and retains heat better than aluminum and stainless steel, food can be prepared at lower temperatures. In fact, Lodge recommends cooking at medium heat for most recipes. Cast iron is a great value. Seasoned properly, cast iron creates its own non-stick coating that more expensive cookware manufacturers brag about.

In recent years, the nutritional benefits of cast iron have come to the attention of experts. Nutritional researchers have documented that cast iron cooking imparts a significant amount of dietary iron into food, which is then absorbed by the body. Some other cookware materials have come under scrutiny, but cast iron has proven to be beneficial to our health.

"Studies indicate cast iron cookware commonly found in American kitchens significantly contributes to the iron content of many cooked foods," says Dr. Craig Walker, a renowned cardiac specialist of The Cardiovascular Institute of The South.

So next time you use that iron skillet, griddle or Dutch oven, remember that by using cast iron, you're getting more than great food cooked well.

NATURAL ◇ HEALTHY COOKING ™

About the Author,
Chef John Folse

Chef John Folse is the owner and executive chef of his Louisiana-based corporations. His Lafitte's Landing Restaurant in Donaldsonville, is recognized as one of the finest restaurants in and around New Orleans. White Oak Plantation, in Baton Rouge, houses his catering and events management company. Louisiana's Premier Products, his cook and chill plant in New Orleans, manufactures soups, sauces, entrees and meats for foodservice and retail establishments across the country. Chef Folse is the author of numerous books and publications available in bookstores nationally.

John is respected around the world as an authority on Cajun and Creole cuisine and culture. He hosts his own national television cooking show, "A Taste of Louisiana" on PBS. In addition, his syndicated radio show, "Stirrin' It Up!," can be heard on many stations nationwide. He has taken his famous "Taste of Louisiana" from Hollywood to the Great Wall of China, opening

promotional Louisiana restaurants in Hong Kong, Japan, Beijing, London, Paris, Rome, Bogota, Taipei and Seoul. In 1987, Chef Folse was selected as "Louisiana Restaurateur of the Year" by the Louisiana Restaurant Association and in November of 1988, the Louisiana Sales and Marketing Executives named him "Louisiana's Marketing Ambassador to the World." In 1988, Chef Folse made international headlines by opening his "Lafitte's Landing East" in Moscow

during the presidential summit between Ronald Reagan and Mikhail Gorbachev. This opening represented the first time an American Restaurant had operated on Soviet soil. Immediately following this venture, John hosted ten Soviet chefs for the first Soviet American Culinary Exchange. In 1989, Chef Folse was invited to create the first ever Vatican State Dinner in Rome, and while there had a private audience with Pope John Paul II. In 1990, Chef Folse was named the "National Chef of the Year" by the American Culinary Federation, the highest honor bestowed upon an American chef. His Lafitte's Landing Restaurant was inducted into the "Fine Dining Hall of Fame," in 1989, and received the DiRoNA (Distinguished Restaurants of North America) award in 1996.

Chef Folse is the recipient of numerous culinary awards and recognitions, and has been honored by local, state and international governments for his continuing efforts to showcase America's regional cooking around the world. His most prestigious acknowledgement to date was Nicholls State University's decision to name their new culinary program in his honor. An Associate of Science in Culinary Arts degree program began in January of 1996, with a Bachelor of Science in Culinary Arts degree program beginning in January of 1997. Nicholls State, his Alma Mater, is located in Thibodaux, Louisiana. For additional information on our organization you may locate us on the Internet at http:\ \www.jfolse.com

"Square Grate with Circular Opening—with Summer Front"
From a 1920s Lodge Cast Iron Catalog

Seasoning Cast Iron:

For many people, the only cast iron they own is a favorite skillet or treasured pan that has been passed down from one generation to the next. These wonderfully aged pieces already have the smooth black patina that gives cast iron its unique cooking surface. But cast iron doesn't come with that look, and new users need to know how to "season" their new pieces.

Seasoning, the process whereby the pores in cast iron absorb oil and create a natural non-stick finish, is not complicated and shouldn't discourage first-time cast iron users.

According to Billie Hill, customer service representative at Lodge Manufacturing, seasoning takes only a few minutes and a little know-how.

"Many young cooks are afraid to buy a new iron skillet because they're worried they might ruin it," Hill says. "But seasoning isn't complicated if you just follow the right steps and keep in mind that all cast iron pieces should be seasoned the same way." According to Hill, the following steps will get any nervous cook off to a good start.

In order to start the process, wash, rinse and thoroughly dry the new skillet to remove the protective wax coating.

2. Put a tablespoon of solid vegetable shortening in utensil. Do not use salted fat (such as margarine or butter). Warm the utensil to melt the shortening then use a cloth or paper towel to coat the entire surface of the utensil, inside and out—including all corners, edges and lids—with the oil.

3. Heat the cookware upside down at 350 degrees for one hour. Be sure to lay aluminum foil on your oven bottom or place a cookie sheet on the rack below to catch any drippings. Turning the piece upside down prevents the oil from building up inside the pan.

4. Remove from oven and wipe with a paper towel. This completes the seasoning process, and you are ready to use your nicely seasoned cast iron.

"Of course there is another way," Hill says. "Fry only bacon in a new skillet for a month or so. Don't wash the pan after each use except with hot water and a brush and then wipe completely dry. I imagine any self-respecting doctor would discourage eating bacon every day for a month, but it does wonders for an iron skillet."

Because detergents can remove seasoning, Hill suggests cleaning cast iron cookware with only hot water and a good stiff brush. But even well seasoned pieces need some attention every now and again.

"Seasoning is a process," Hill says. "The more you use cast iron, the better it gets, but if your pan doesn't have a shiny finish, you should repeat the seasoning process. I like to smile at my cast iron, and if it doesn't smile back, I know I need to re-season."

In addition to seasoning, the general care of cast iron is also important. By following these easy steps, you can ensure your cast iron pieces will be around to serve you for a long time to come.

1. Always wash with a mild detergent, rinse and dry thoroughly. Never scour or use a dishwasher. (You may use a plastic bun to remove stubborn food particles.)

2. Cook food with little water content the first few times. Avoid cooking acidic foods such as tomatoes, unless combined with other foods. Uncover hot food as you remove from the heat, because steam may remove the protective coating.

3. Rust, a metallic taste or discolored foods are signs of improper or inadequate seasoning. If this occurs, wash thoroughly and re-season.

4. Since cast iron heats evenly, it is not necessary to use extremely high cooking temperatures. Best results are obtained with medium to medium-to-high temperature settings. Do not overheat or leave empty utensil on burner. Never place utensil on an already heated burner; rather, allow the utensil to heat as the burner does.

5. Always store cast iron utensils with tops or lids off so moisture won't collect inside. Store in a warm, dry place. A paper towel placed inside the utensil will absorb any moisture and prevent rust.

6. For best results, warm cast iron utensils in the oven while preparing ingredients. This will ensure that food cooks evenly without sticking.

That black finish that good cooks covet will develop over time, generating years of good cooking and creating a new heirloom for future generations.

A Page *from* Our Past...

From a 1920s Lodge Cast Iron Catalog

Chapter 1

New England

The influence of New England cuisine on today's menus is quite evident as we see steamed lobster, clam chowder, meat pies, and a collection of other delectable items. From the mountainous and coastal regions of New England we are blessed with superb ingredients for our iron pots.

Although a variety of explorers visited the New England coast, it was the English Puritans who landed at Plymouth Rock in December of 1690 and who succeeded with their settlement there. This land, rugged and fertile, was quite unlike the land the Puritans had left behind in England. Luckily, the newcomers were acclimated by the Algonkian Indians who were compassionate enough to teach these pilgrims how to hunt, fish, plant and farm in this strange new land.

The Indian foods such as hominy, succotash, hoecakes, roasted corn and popcorn became a novelty to the English. They enjoyed pumpkin bread, tarts, carrots, turnips, cucumbers, green peas, butter, candied fruit, berries, apple cider, roasted turkey, boiled seafood and game, and fresh herbs. Cookery at first was ingenious adaptations of the Indian food. The Puritans dined on pumpkin as a staple in their diets. From their homeland, they brought herbs and planted them for use to make the meats more suited to the English tastes. One early Indian dish still very popular today is the New England Succotash, which combines corn, beans, chicken, beef and salt pork into a hearty stew.

Other immigrants came to the New England area, but few stayed and made an impact on the cookery of the region. Two exceptions to this were the Polish, who contributed their garlic sausage Kielbasy and bakery items, and the Shakers, who arrived in 1774 and introduced remarkably modern cooking methods. These methods included vegetables cooked in little water and meatless dishes using mushrooms, lentils, rice, cheese, fruits and vegetables.

The French Canadians, who arrived in the late 1800s, were not so displaced as the early Pilgrims, so their cuisine was much like the people, a hearty blend of French, New England and

Canadian influence. Their split pea and cheese soups remain popular and their renowned meat pies are uniquely New England.

The English are known for their boiled dinner, which is widely misunderstood, as it is truly simmered and not boiled. Pot roast, for example, is simmered in water, herbs and vegetables. Large iron pots were characteristic of the English kitchens and used to boil game meats and roast beef.

Still, the most recognized dishes in the New England region are the New England Boiled Dinner and New England Succotash, along with Boston's Baked Beans, Maine's Clam Chowders and Boiled Lobsters. One pot meals that "cook themselves" were the order of the day centuries ago, and these dishes of the region are still easy to prepare and popular worldwide today.

Chef James Griffin

Born in Gloucester, Massachusetts, Chef James Griffin graduated from the culinary arts program at Johnson & Wales University in 1986 and completed a Bachelor of Science degree in food service management in 1988.

During his tenure at Johnson and Wales, Griffin completed three years of training with Chef George Karousos at the Ivy Award winning Sea Fare Inn in Portsmouth, Rhode Island. He then went on to serve as executive chef at Hutchins and Wheeler in Boston and at Lambert's Cove Country Inn in West Tisbury, Massachusetts.

In 1990, Griffin returned to Johnson & Wales to teach cooking, and in 1992 completed a Master of Science degree in hospitality administration. In 1995, he was awarded the prestigious Robert Nograd Teacher of

the Year Award at Johnson & Wales. He has also been awarded the gold medal of honor and four gold medals by the New England chapters of the American Culinary Federation. He is a member of the 1996 U.S. Culinary Team and earned the highest national cold score at the recent U.S. Culinary Team try-outs, earning a 38.3 out of a possible 40 points.

Chef Griffin has always possessed a passion for creative cooking and finds the New England traditions a creative outlet; a unique blend of indigenous foods, native culture and new cuisine from the European immigrants.

It is well known that Native Americans lived off the land—reaping the benefits of plentiful Northeast crops such as corn and winter squash. They also relied on the abundant varieties of fish easily caught in the coastal waters. When the English Puritan settlers arrived, they brought with them traditional fare. Sheep and hogs were common meat sources, while dairy cows introduced cream and cheeses to the area. While the immigrants were partially adept at adjusting to their new surroundings, they did seek help from the Native Americans and learned to blend the two cooking styles.

As one might imagine, fish, such as flounder, cod and sole, were important to everyone in the Northeast, not only as sustenance but also as a source of revenue. Today it continues to be a rich part of the region's culinary heritage.

The result, according to Chef Griffin, is basic and functional foods that can be prepared quickly and inexpensively. In fact, lobster and crab bisque, considered a luxurious delicacy in other parts of the country are almost mundane and repetitive fare to Northeastern natives.

And while regional cuisine is constantly changing as a result of increasing ethnicity, foods such as chowders, stews, fruits and beans are still considered mainstays in the Northeast.

"My great grandmother gave my grandmother her cast iron skillet that was seasoned with pork fat. She used flint white corn meal to make a really dense corn bread. In our family, it's a tradition that the best cook gets that pan. I now have that pan, and it's one of my favorites."

Ipswich Fried Clams

The sweet clams from the Essex River near Ipswich, Massachusetts, are well worth the investment.

Ingredients:

8 cups Ipswich softshell clams, shucked and cleaned
2 cups corn flour
1 tsp salt
1 tsp pepper
1 quart vegetable oil

Strain the clams and reserve juice for later use. In a large mixing bowl, combine corn flour, salt and pepper. In a 12-inch cast iron skillet, place the vegetable oil over medium-high heat. Dredge clams, 8-10 at a time, into the corn flour mixture until the clams are completely covered. Drop clams into the oil and fry until golden brown. Remove clams and drain on paper towels. Continue until all clams are fried. Serve with tartar sauce.
Prep Time: 30 Minutes   **Serves**: 6

"Polished Hollow Ware—Dutch Oven with Legs"
From a 1920s Lodge Cast Iron Catalog

Cast iron . . . the ultimate non-stick!

Gloucester Fish Chowder

A traditional white fish chowder from the fishing community of Gloucester, Massachusetts.

Ingredients:

4 pounds cod, fresh cheeks
   or tail trim
1 ounce salt pork, rinsed
2 slices bacon
1 large onion, diced
3 cups peeled potatoes, diced
   1/2-inch thick

8 cups skim milk
1/2 tsp salt
1/2 tsp pepper
1/2 tsp thyme

Place the salt pork, fat side down, in a 10-quart cast iron Dutch oven over medium-high heat. Heat salt pork until the fat melts into 1 tablespoon of liquid. Add bacon and fry until golden brown and crispy. Remove pork and bacon and place on paper towels to drain. Set aside. Into the same Dutch oven, place onions. Saute until onions are tender, approximately 3-5 minutes. Add potatoes and milk. Bring mixture to a rolling boil, reduce heat to simmer and cook for 15 minutes. Add fish and simmer an additional 15 minutes. Using a slotted spoon, stir the soup in order to break up fish. Season to taste with salt, pepper and thyme. Allow chowder to simmer an additional 10 minutes. Garnish with unsalted crackers or crumbled French bread.

Prep Time: 45 Minutes   **Serves:** 6

 Cast iron cookware is cheaper per pound thanhamburger meat and lasts a lifetime!

Yankee Pot Roast

A delicious version of the old New England classic.

Ingredients:

4 pounds beef bottom round, trimmed
2 ounces salt pork
1/2 cup flour
8 cups beef stock
1 bay leaf
1 sprig thyme
1 sprig parsley

6 carrots, cut 3-inches in length
6 pearl onions
2 turnip tops, cut into thirds
6 red new potatoes
2 tbsps flour
1 tbsp salt
1 tbsp black pepper

In a 10-quart cast iron Dutch oven, place salt pork over medium high heat. Heat pork until the fat melts into 1 tablespoon of liquid. In a large mixing bowl, place 1/2 cup of flour. Season to taste using salt and pepper. Season roast well using salt and pepper and dust in flour. Sear the roast on all sides in the hot oil. Add beef stock, bay leaf, thyme and parsley. Bring mixture to a rolling boil, reduce heat to simmer and cover. Cook for approximately 3 hours. Add carrots, onions and turnips. Simmer for an additional 30 minutes. Add potatoes and cook 30 minutes. Remove the meat to a cutting board and keep warm. Strain liquid, reserving vegetables and stock. Pour stock into Dutch oven and bring to a rolling boil. Sprinkle in flour and blend until sauce is creamy, approximately 15 minutes. Slice roast and arrange in the center of serving platter, surrounded by vegetables. Top with gravy and serve warm. Serve with fresh baked bread (to sop up the sauce!).
Prep Time: 4 1/2 Hours   **Serves:** 6

Cast iron is made in a sand-casting process.

Acorn Squash *with* Sugar & Cranberries

A late harvest favorite, squash is an excellent complement to poultry, game and pork dishes.

Ingredients:

3 acorn squash,
    peeled and seeded
1/2 cup brown sugar
1/2 cup cranberries
1/4 cup butter

1 cup diced onion
1/4 cup chopped parsley
1 cup chicken stock
1/2 tsp salt
1/2 tsp pepper

Preheat oven to 350 degrees F. Dice squash into 1/2-inch cubes. In a 12-inch cast iron skillet, melt butter over medium-high heat. Add squash and saute 2-3 minutes. Add sugar, cranberries, onion and parsley. Saute until onions are wilted, approximately 3-5 minutes. Add chicken stock and season to taste using salt and pepper. Cover, place in oven and bake for 25 minutes or until squash is tender. Serve immediately.

Prep Time: 1 Hour   **Serves:** 6

10-Quart Dutch Oven
From the current Lodge Cast Iron Catalog

Apple Maple Tart Tatin

This dish combines two traditional New England ingredients — apples and maple syrup — for a unique flavor treat.

Ingredients for Filling:

6 Corland or Fuji apples
3/4 cup maple syrup
2 tbsp lemon juice
1/4 cup butter

1/2 cup sugar
1/4 cup flour
1/2 tsp cinnamon

Ingredients for Dough:

2 cups flour
1/2 cup butter
1 egg

pinch of sugar
1/2 tsp salt
3 tsps milk

Preheat oven to 400 degrees F. Peel and core apples. Cut into quarters and sprinkle with lemon juice. Set aside. In a 12-inch cast iron skillet, melt butter over medium-high heat. Dust the bottom of the skillet with 1/2 cup sugar until completely covered. Remove from heat and set aside. In a large mixing bowl, place apples, syrup, 1/4 cup of flour and cinnamon. Toss apples coating completely with syrup mixture. Line the bottom of the skillet with apples in a decorative fashion. To prepare pie dough, place 2 cups of flour on a flat surface. Cut in butter. Add egg, sugar and salt. Knead dough until it forms a ball. Add milk and knead several times until smooth. Roll dough into a 1/4-inch thick circle, large enough to cover the skillet. Place the dough over the apples and trim away the excess dough. Place the skillet over medium heat. When the edges of the pan begin to bubble, remove skillet. Place tart in oven and bake for 15 minutes or until the crust is brown. Carefully turn hot tart over onto a large serving platter. Allow tart to cool slightly before serving.

Prep Time: 1 Hour   **Serves:** 6

Columbus brought cast iron with him to the New World in 1492.

A Page *from* Our Past . . .

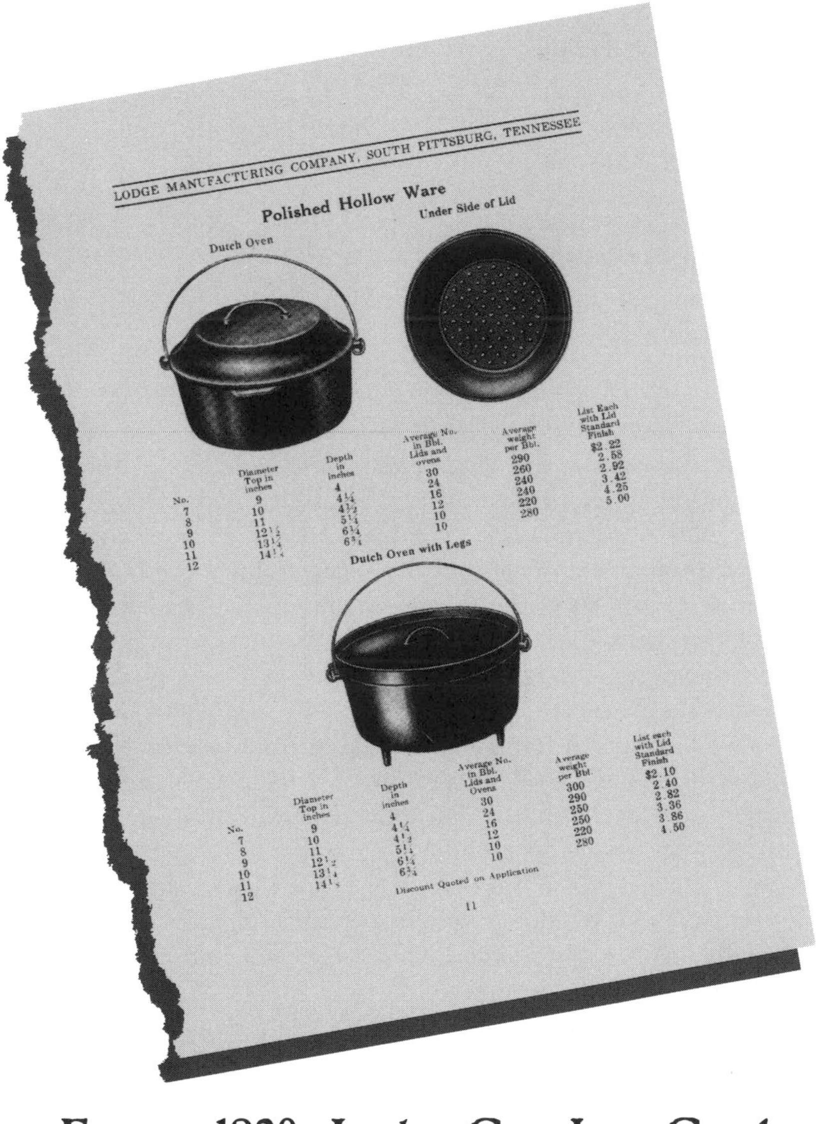

LODGE MANUFACTURING COMPANY, SOUTH PITTSBURG, TENNESSEE

Polished Hollow Ware

Dutch Oven

Under Side of Lid

No.	Diameter Top in inches	Depth in inches	Average No. in Bbl. Lids and ovens	Average weight per Bbl.	List Each with Lid Standard Finish
7	9	4	30	290	$2.22
8	10	4¼	24	260	2.58
9	11	4½	16	240	2.92
10	12½	5¼	12	240	3.42
11	13¼	6¼	10	220	4.25
12	14½	6¾	10	280	5.00

Dutch Oven with Legs

No.	Diameter Top in inches	Depth in inches	Average No. in Bbl. Lids and Ovens	Average weight per Bbl.	List each with Lid Standard Finish
7	9	4	30	300	$2.10
8	10	4¼	24	290	2.40
9	11	4½	16	250	2.82
10	12½	5¼	12	250	3.36
11	13¼	6¼	10	220	3.86
12	14½	6¾	10	280	4.50

Discount Quoted on Application

11

From a 1920s Lodge Cast Iron Catalog

A Page *from* Our Past . . .

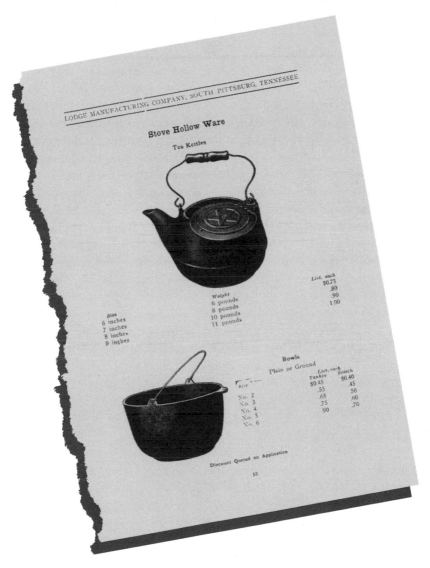

LODGE MANUFACTURING COMPANY, SOUTH PITTSBURG, TENNESSEE

Stove Hollow Ware

Tea Kettles

Size	Weight	List, each
6 inches	6 pounds	$0.75
7 inches	8 pounds	.80
8 inches	10 pounds	.90
9 inches	11 pounds	1.00

Bowls
Plain or Ground

Size	List, each Yankee	Scotch
No. 2	$0.45	$0.40
No. 3	.55	.45
No. 4	.65	.50
No. 5	.75	.60
No. 6	.90	.70

Discount Quoted on Application

15

From a 1920s Lodge Cast Iron Catalog

Chapter 2
Low Country

Low Country or Low Lands Cuisine defines one that is strikingly similar to that of South Louisiana, with rice serving as the principal ingredient in many recipes. The Charleston area of South Carolina is the heart of the low country, though many will agree that its influences extend into North Carolina and Georgia.

The Cherokee, Catawba and Yamasee Indians occupied the area before the first white settlers appeared from Spain and England to establish the plantations of rice, cotton, tobacco and indigo. The most widely accepted date of settlement is 1670. Other immigrant populations to settle the low country region include the French and Germans. Many early gentry settlers came from plantations in the Caribbean bringing with them the spices of Barbados and other islands. These spices, such as hot bird's eye peppers, mace and nutmeg add intense flavors of the tropics to this region's cuisine.

The topography of the low lands region consists of a riverain-estuarial environment with a climate mild and humid and rainfall averaging 50 inches annually. Game and wildlife such as white-tailed deer, rabbit, raccoon, wild turkey, duck and quail are abundant. Neighboring the Atlantic Ocean, trapping and fishing are critical to the culture, and the delicate seafoods of oysters, shrimp and crabs bring unique flavors to the pot.

Okra is widely used in low country cooking as is rice, which can be considered the defining staple ingredient and the leading crop as of the late 17th century. Rice is seen in numerous dishes including a most popular dish somewhat similar to jambalaya, rice pilau. This dish, which has many variations, can also be compared to oriental pilaf. Corn is another essential ingredient in this cuisine, used simply in corn bread or eaten daily at breakfast in the form of hominy, and served in various souffle and pudding recipes.

The low country is famous for its "hoppin' john" — a must for New Years Day but popular any time of the year. Again, we can draw a similarity to South Louisiana where black-eyed peas are served alongside cabbage and corned beef brisket on January 1.

The vast ingredients of the low country region come together to create wonderful, memorable recipes. One of the most elegant of their seafood dishes is the She-Crab Soup, a creamed-based soup using the orange roe of female crabs to add to its richness and finished with a touch of sherry. Shrimp and other seafoods are even seen at the breakfast table, where they are served as a spiced paste blend and spread on toast. Along with seafood, rice and corn meal dishes by far dominate and define the low country menu.

Chef Don McMillan

Chef Don McMillan learned his culinary trade by working aboard merchant vessels and yachts. In each of the 39 countries to which he traveled, he learned the local cooking techniques and mastered the art of menu formation and recipe development.

He began an impressive career that included 16 years with ARA Services in food service management. During his tenure there, he was responsible for volume food service administration at venues including Denver's Mile High Stadium, the Denver Art Museum, and the 1980 Winter Olympics in Lake Placid, New York.

After settling in the Carolinas, he became very involved in the community, serving two terms as president of the Triad Chapter of the American Culinary Federation (ACF); as a member of the executive board of directors of the Greater Winston-Salem Chamber of Commerce; and as a member of the Forsyth County Restaurant Association. He also serves as chairman of "Chef and the Child," an ACF program designed to teach nutrition to children in five North Carolina counties, and was named Entrepreneur of the

Year by the local Chamber of Commerce.

Today, he is the chef and owner of Simple Elegance, a corporation that includes two restaurants, a catering company and a cooking school. He is also the host of "Monday's Menu," a weekly cooking segment on Winston Salem's NBC affiliate.

Chef McMillan's vast experience in the Carolina Lowlands have made him a regional expert on the foods representative of the Carolina Lowlands. The Lowlands, which extend from Norfolk to near Hilton Head, produce the shrimp, crabs and other seafood available on the coast; however, Carolina foods are also derived from the mountain regions.

Settlers of the area used what they could catch—from seafood to indigenous game, such as squirrel and rabbit. In the summer they enjoyed fresh vegetables, but in the winter they survived on dried corn, rice and nuts, water cress and greens. Their favorite recipes changed from season to season based on what was available.

In his cooking school, Chef McMillan encourages students to aim for simplicity in their menus. Ingredients should be easy to find and preparation instructions should be easy to follow.

"My father would never eat fish unless it was served with corn bread, because he was certain the bones would stick in his throat, if he didn't eat bread with his meal. He called it hoe cake, because in the old days they cooked it in the field on a hoe over a fire. Today, the best hoe cake is prepared in a cast iron skillet because it cooks evenly with no hot spots."

3-Piece Skillet Set
From a current Lodge Cast Iron Catalog

26

Brunswick Stew

This hunter's stew has as many recipes as there are cooks. This complete meal in a pot is cooked over an open fire and includes meat from the day's hunting such as rabbit or squirrel. Dry vegetables such as beans and corn and cured meat such as country ham are almost always included. In this recipe I have made this recipe more user-friendly by replacing the game with chicken. I have found some form of Brunswick Stew offered throughout the mountain regions of the Southeast.

Ingredients:

3 pounds chicken thighs
2 tbsps salad oil
1 cup diced country ham
3 quarts chicken stock
1 large onion, chopped
1 1/2 cups fresh or frozen
    baby lima beans
1 bay leaf
2 hot peppers, diced
4 medium potatoes,
    peeled and cubed

2 pounds fresh tomatoes,
    peeled and seeded
1 tsp thyme
1 tsp sugar
1 1/2 tbsps salt
1/2 tsp black pepper
3 cups fresh corn
2 tbsps butter
1 tbsp Worcestershire sauce

In a 10-quart cast iron Dutch oven, heat oil over medium-high heat. Add chicken and saute until golden brown on both sides. Add ham and stock. Bring mixture to a rolling boil, reduce to simmer and cook for 1 hour. Add onion, lima beans, bay leaf, hot peppers, potatoes, tomatoes, thyme, sugar, salt and pepper. Cover and simmer for 45 minutes. Add corn and cook, uncovered, for 15 minutes. Adjust seasonings if necessary. When ready to serve, swirl in butter and Worcestershire sauce. Serve in soup bowls with hot corn bread.

Prep Time: 2 1/2 Hours   **Serves:** 8

Cast iron is the oldest cookware known to man.

Spoon Bread

Southern cooks prepare a variety of breads. Corn meal is a prominent grain used in baking because of its availability and popularity. Spoon bread is a lighter version of typical corn bread, because of the beaten egg whites used in the recipe. Carolinians prefer their corn bread unsweetened unlike its Northern counterpart, which uses sugar and is often consumed at breakfast. It's interesting that we Southerners prefer corn bread with our meals rather than fresh baked wheat or rye varieties.

Ingredients:

2 cups whole milk
1/2 cup corn meal
1 tsp salt

2 tbsps melted butter
2 eggs, separated
1/2 tsp baking powder

Preheat oven to 400 degrees F. Grease a 12-inch cast iron skillet and place in hot oven. In a 3-quart cast iron sauce pan, heat milk until simmering. Gradually add corn meal and salt to the hot milk, stirring constantly. Continue to blend until corn meal has absorbed the milk and becomes stiff. Add butter, blend well and remove from heat. In a separate bowl, place egg yolks and baking powder. Using an electric mixer, beat until well blended. Pour egg mixture into corn meal batter. Blend well and set aside. In a separate mixing bowl, beat egg whites until stiff. Using a large serving spoon, gently fold egg whites into the batter. Pour batter into preheated 12-inch skillet and bake for 35 minutes. Bread will be done when firm to the touch and golden brown.

Prep Time: 1 Hour   **Serves**:   6

Cast iron is corn bread's best friend.

Moravian Chicken Pie

The Moravians were early settlers in the North Carolina Piedmont region. Their lifestyle was simple and their cuisine, handed down through the generations, still demonstrates this quality. The chicken pie enjoyed today in the Triad area consist of chicken, broth and a flaky pie dough topping. Prior to sitting down to this wonderful meal, why not join hands and recite this MORAVIAN BLESSING: Come Lord Jesus, our Guest to be, And bless these gifts bestowed by Thee. Amen.

Ingredients:

1 (4-pound) chicken poached,
   reserve liquid
1 cup flour
1/4 tsp salt
1/2 cup butter
2 1/2 tbsps cold water

3 tbsps butter
3 tbsps flour
3 cups reserved stock
2 tbsps butter
1/2 tsp salt
1/2 tsp pepper

NOTE: To poach, quarter chicken. Place the chicken in a small stock pot and add 1 quartered onion, 1 sliced carrot, 1 bay leaf and a pinch of salt and pepper. Cover with water by 3 inches. Bring liquid to a rolling boil, reduce to low simmer and cook until chicken is tender, approximately 30 minutes. Remove the chicken from the poaching liquid and set aside to cool slightly. Strain and reserve 3 cups of chicken stock. Skin and debone the chicken. Cut the meat into 1-inch pieces and set aside. Preheat oven to 400 degrees F. In a mixing bowl, sift flour and 1/4 teaspoon salt together. Cut in butter until the mixture resembles corn meal. Quickly stir in the cold water and turn mixture out onto a floured surface. Knead until smooth and form into a circle. Wrap dough in plastic wrap and refrigerate for 1/2 hour. In a 10-inch cast iron skillet, melt 3 tablespoons of butter over medium-high heat. Sprinkle in flour and, using a wire whisk, stir until light brown roux is achieved. Slowly add reserved chicken stock, a little at a time, until rich stew-like consistency is achieved. Add chicken meat, blending well into the stew mixture. Season to taste using salt and pepper. Remove from heat and set aside. Grease another 10-inch cast iron skillet. Pour chicken mixture into the skillet and distribute evenly across the bottom. Remove dough from the refrigerator and roll out into a 12-inch circle, approximately 1/4-

inch thick. Place dough over chicken mixture, crimping the edges around the top of the skillet. Using a paring knife, cut several steam vents around top of pastry. Bake 10-12 minutes and reduce temperature to 350 degrees F. Bake until pastry is golden brown, approximately 30 minutes.

Prep Time: 2 Hours **Serves:** 6

Gullah Rice

In pre-TV days, my father would entertain his "young-uns" with tales from the Carolinas, from the mountains and its "hillbillies" to the shore "Sea Islands" where the "Gullahs" lived. The Gullahs were freed slaves from West Africa who developed their own spoken language, though not written. My father called it "geechie". The Gullahs were great fisherman and harvested rice. In fact, an important dish in their native kitchen is Jolof rice. I later learned that the name of this dish was changed to red rice, due to the red spices added for fiery flavor. I remember my father telling me of an old GULLAH PROVERB: Promising talk don't cook rice.

Ingredients:

2 cups uncooked rice
2 pounds smoked sausage, sliced
   1/2-inch thick
1 cup chopped onion
1 cup chopped red bell pepper
1-2 chopped hot peppers

1 tsp brown sugar
1 tsp salt
1 cup chopped tomatoes
2 1/2 cups chicken stock
1 cup cooked black beans

In a 10-quart cast iron Dutch oven, brown sausage over medium-high heat. Remove, drain and set aside. Remove all oil from Dutch oven except for 4 tablespoons. Add onion, bell peppers and hot peppers. Saute until vegetables are wilted, approximately 3-5 minutes. Add rice and stir to coat the grains with vegetable mixture. Stir in sausage, sugar, salt and tomatoes. Pour in chicken stock, one ladle at a time, blending well. Bring mixture to a rolling boil, reduce heat to simmer and cover. Cook for 20 minutes. Remove Dutch oven from heat. Stir in black beans, cover and let stand for 10 minutes. Serve warm.

Prep Time: 45 Minutes **Serves:** 6

 Cast iron is noted for its even heat distribution.

30

North Carolina Hillbilly Apple Sonker

This cobbler-like dessert is found in the mountains and foothills of North Carolina. Traditionally, fresh fruit is used as the base — wild blackberries, peaches, apples or combinations thereof. The crust is made flaky by using butter or shortening although lard was the original fat used in pastry making. Vinegar is added for additional flavor and whole egg for richness. Whenever making pie crust, it's always a great idea to make one or two for the freezer. This ensures that there will always be a crust ready when berries are available with little or no notice.

Ingredients:

12 apples, peeled and cored
2 tbsps butter
2 cups sugar
1/2 cup flour

1/2 tsp cinnamon
1 cup whipping cream
1/2 cup sugar
1 tsp vanilla

Preheat oven to 400 degrees F. Lightly grease a 10-inch cast iron skillet. In a large mixing bowl, place apples, sugar, flour and cinnamon. Toss lightly to coat apples with sugar mixture. Place apples into skillet and top with pastry crust. (recipe follows) Using a paring knife, cut 1-inch steam holes in the top of the pastry for ventilation. Bake sonker for 40 minutes or until crust is golden brown and flaky. Remove from oven and cool slightly. In the bowl of an electric mixer, place whipping cream, 1/2 cup sugar and vanilla. Beat on high speed until soft peaks form. Using a serving spoon, place a generous portion of the sonker in the center of an 8-inch plate and top with fresh whipped cream.
Prep Time: 1 1/2 Hours   **Serves:** 8

Ingredients for Dough:

1 whole egg
10 tbsps tap water
2 tsps vinegar

3 cups all purpose flour
1 tsp salt
3/4 cup shortening or butter

In the bowl of an electric mixer, beat egg, water and vinegar. In a large mixing bowl, sift together flour and salt. Using your hands, crumble the shortening or butter into the flour mixture, blending thoroughly until mixture resembles the texture of corn meal. Pour

31

in water mixture and blend until dough forms. Turn the dough out onto a lightly floured surface and knead until smooth. Divide into 3 equal portions and roll each crust into a circle until 1/4-inch thick. You may freeze two of the crust by wrapping in wax paper and placing in a Ziplock bag for later use. **Makes:** 3 Pie Crusts

Cast iron skillets are born one at time — each in a different sand mold.

A Page *from* Our Past . . .

From a 1920s Lodge Cast Iron Catalog

Chapter 3
The Caribbean

With thousands of islands, some inhabited, some not, comprising what is known as the Caribbean, it is no wonder that an extensive variety of ingredients must come together to classify the Caribbean cuisine.

The Caribbean islands are surrounded by the Gulf of Mexico, Atlantic Ocean, Caribbean Sea and the Yucatan Channel. Their dishes have been influenced by the British, Dutch, Portuguese, Chinese, French, Spanish, East Indian, Native American and West African cultures. With its unique spices, peppers and tropical fruits and vegetables, Caribbean cuisine takes on a personality like no other.

It was Christopher Columbus who discovered the Caribbean in 1492 during his quest for the spices of India. In 1493, he found pineapple, an essential ingredient to this cuisine, on the island of Guadeloupe. The papaya, another Caribbean fruit, was also discovered and is used today as a condiment, its leaves as a meat tenderizer.

The unique tropical climate and landscapes allow for lush gardens of vegetation, including plants found on these islands alone. A few ingredients which are seen repeatedly in Caribbean recipes include cassava, batata, pumpkin, papaya, banana and pineapple. Other ingredients considered essential to the Caribbean cook are local chile peppers, okra, rum, nutmeg, cinnamon and Jamaican Jerk. Jamaican Jerk is an important seasoning in island cooking which was created as many of the local ingredients, such as chilis and spices, were married together. The varied fish and seafood of the islands are also key to the successful preparation of this cuisine.

The Natives were known to eat grouper, snapper and shrimp from the rivers and oceans. They also cultivated the vegetable crops on the islands and passed along their in-depth knowledge of chile peppers to the settlers that followed. The British introduced potatoes, rice pudding, kidney pie and smoked herring. French cooking methods can be seen today in St. Martin,

Martinique and Guadeloupe, while the Spanish cuisine is most prominent in Cuba, Puerto Rico and the Dominican Republic. The Spanish Paella, the foundation of the Louisiana jambalaya, is still a local favorite.

The West African influence is evident in the popular dish called Cou-Cou, which is found mostly on the island of Barbados and contains corn meal and okra. Chinese brought with them their stir-fry methods and sweet and sour sauces, which are now a required element of Caribbean cooking. With the East Indians, the Caribbean gained wheat, flour, rice, curries, mangoes, eggplants and ginger. Pelau, a popular dish in Trinidad, is of East Indian origin.

For an exciting treat of tropical dishes that is sure to be spicy and satisfying, a visit to the Caribbean or just a dinner comprised of the fabulous Caribbean recipes in this book, is a sure winner.

Chef Andre Niederhauser

Chef Andre Neiderhauser began his career in Switzerland but quickly expanded his culinary horizons in England, Bermuda, the United States and Jamaica. For the last 10 years, he has honed his skills in Caribbean cuisine as owner, manager and chef of some of the best hotels and restaurants in Jamaica.

Today he is the owner and chef of the Restaurant Temple Hall Estates, the only recipient of the "Best of the Caribbean's" Three Silver Star Award of Excellence in Jamaica. He is also responsible for establishing Lillian's, a restaurant school, and consults for Darden Restaurants, the restaurant business division of General Mills. The specialty dishes he creates are as flavorful and varied as the Caribbean culture.

Caribbean cuisine evolved as the original inhabitants of the area, Arawaks and Caribs, began to share their home with West Africans, English, French, Dutch, Spainards, Portuguese, Chinese and Indians. After the discovery of India, the gates of the Caribbean were opened to traders and settlers, and the diverse culinary influences of these visitors to the area resulted in new and interesting dishes.

Like the Indians, Caribs relied heavily on smoking as a method of food preservation and continue to appreciate the simplicity of coal cooking. The natives also combined the new ingredients and methods of preparation they discovered from their new neighbors.

As labor from Asia and Africa came to the area, so came another dimension to an already wide selection of culinary delicacies. Finally, the growing tourist market, diversified in origin, required creative adaptations—using imported and local ingredients to satisfy both the visitors' tastes and expectations.

These influences, coupled with the utilization of modern equipment as well as the addition of Chef Neiderhauser's own creativity, has resulted in a wonderful evolution and emerging identity for what has become Caribbean cuisine.

Paella del Caribe

My Spanish ancestors considered paella one of the most elegant dishes that could be placed on a table. Naturally, every region of the world has its interpretation of this rice dish. This recipe is a favorite of most people living on the Spanish-speaking islands.

Ingredients:

1/2 cup conch
1/2 cup (70-90 count) shrimp, peeled and deveined
2 (7-ounce) fish fillets, cubed
1 cup breast of chicken, diced
1/4 cup olive oil
1 tsp saffron
1 cup onions, diced
1 cup tomato, diced
1 cup carrots, diced

12 young okra, whole
1 quart chicken stock
1 bay leaf
2 whole cloves
2 sprigs of thyme
1/4 cup sliced green onions
1/4 cup chopped parsley
1 tbsp lime juice
salt and black pepper
2 cups long grain rice

In a 15-inch cast iron skillet, heat olive oil over medium-high heat. Add seafoods and chicken, a little at a time, until all are sauteed and cooked approximately medium rare to medium. Add saffron, onions, tomato and carrots. Saute 3-5 minutes or until vegetables are wilted. The saffron will give the dish a wonderful golden color and a unique flavor. Add okra, chicken stock, bay leaves, cloves and thyme. Bring mixture to a rolling boil, blend well into the seasonings and meat, and reduce heat to simmer. Add green onions, parsley and lime juice. Season to taste using salt and pepper. Stir in long grain rice, blending well into the seafood mixture. Cover and cook 30-45 minutes, stirring at 15-minute intervals. Serve as a main dish.

Prep Time: 1 Hour   **Serves:** 6

Lewis & Clark carried cast iron cookware on their expedition to the Pacific N.W. in 1804.

Curried Goat

Often, one culture will inspire unique recipes by adapting its technique and philosophy of cooking to regional ingredients. This classic Caribbean dish was created by the East Indians, who found great joy in using island flavors with their curry. This Island/Indian dish is normally served over steamed white rice.

Ingredients:

3 pounds goat meat, cubed
2 tsps curry
2 tbsps grated ginger
1 ounce lime juice
1 tbsp salt
1/2 cup coconut oil
1/4 cup granulated sugar

1 cup diced onions
2 tbsps chopped garlic
1 tbsp chopped thyme
1 cup tomato sauce
1/2 cup water
1 cup coconut milk
salt and pepper

Rinse the goat thoroughly and place in a large ceramic bowl. Top with ginger, lime juice and salt. Blend well and allow to sit at room temperature for 4 hours. In a 7-quart cast iron Dutch oven, heat coconut oil over medium-high heat. Add sugar and stir constantly until well blended. The sugar should cook until slightly golden, but not quite to the caramel state. Add goat and cook slowly until meat is golden brown. Do not stir often, in order to allow the meat to caramelize well in the bottom of the pot. Add onions, garlic, thyme and curry. Blend well into the vegetable mixture. Saute 3-5 minutes or until vegetables are wilted. Add tomato sauce, water and coconut milk. Bring to a rolling boil, reduce heat to simmer and cover. Cook until meat is tender, approximately 45 minutes. Season to taste using salt and pepper. Once tender, the dish is normally served with a chutney of diced bananas, papaya, mango, pineapple and grated coconut.

Prep Time: 1 Hour   **Serves:** 6

English Pot
From a 1920s Lodge Cast Iron Catalog

Shrimp & Pumpkin Soup

Unique soups are considered a religious affair in this region of the world. Most of the ingredients are common in the area, but the procedures and techniques are often centuries old. Our five o'clock meal or dinner, as you may know it, was generally a substantial soup of the islands.

Ingredients:

2 pounds (50-60 count) shrimp, peeled and deveined, reserve shells
2 cups diced orange pumpkin, reserve skin
1 onion, halved
3 cloves garlic
1 sprig thyme
1 carrot, sliced
3/4 cup butter
1 cup diced onions
1/2 cup sliced scallions
3/4 cup flour
1/2 tsp jerk seasoning
1 cup heavy whipping cream
salt and black pepper

In a 5-quart cast iron Dutch oven, place shrimp shells, 1 onion, garlic cloves, thyme, carrot and pumpkin skin. Cover contents by 2 inches with cold water. Bring mixture to a rolling boil and reduce to simmer. Cook the stock for 1 hour, strain and reserve 2 quarts of liquid. Discard any remaining vegetables. In the same Dutch oven, melt butter over medium-high heat. Add diced onions, scallions and pumpkin. Saute 3-5 minutes or until vegetables are wilted. Add flour, blending well into the mixture to create a blonde roux. Add 1 quart of reserved stock, a little at a time, until all is incorporated. Blend well and cook until pumpkin is tender, approximately 30 minutes. Place the contents in the bowl of a food processor fitted with a metal blade, and blend until smooth and creamy. Return mixture to the Dutch oven and add remaining stock and half of the shrimp. Add jerk seasoning and bring mixture to a low simmer. Season to taste using salt and pepper. Cook 15-20 minutes. Add heavy whipping cream and adjust seasonings if necessary. Add remaining shrimp, blending thoroughly. Cook 2-3 minutes and serve.

Prep Time: 2 Hours   **Serves:** 6

Cast iron is healthful – it imparts dietary iron into the food which is absorbed by the body.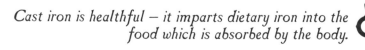

Port Royal Escoweichero Fish

This is a classic pirate recipe from the days when the infamous Captain Morgan had his way around the Caribbean. Although this simple frying technique makes the dish easy to accomplish, the final flavor will make you a superstar. It is best to have your seafood supplier scale and clean your fish thoroughly, but leave the head and tail intact for presentation.

Ingredients:

6 (2 1/2-pound) whole snappers, cleaned
1/2 cup lime juice
4 tbsps black pepper
3 tbsps salt
1 Scotch Bonnet pepper, minced

1/2 cup carrots, julienned
1/2 cup chow chow mix
1 large onion, sliced thin
2 cups red wine vinegar
2 cups coconut oil

Place the fish on a large baking pan and rub with lime juice, pepper and salt. While fish is marinating, place the Scotch Bonnet, carrot, chow chow, onions, and vinegar in a 3-quart cast iron sauce pot. Bring to a low boil and remove from heat. Cool slightly. In a 15-inch cast iron skillet, heat oil over medium-high heat. The oil should reach approximately 375 degrees F. Being careful not to break the fish, fry the fish whole, two at a time, until crispy and fully cooked. Remove and keep warm. Continue until all fish are done. Once fried, top each fish with the spicy carrot vinegar. Serve one fish per person.

Prep Time: 1 Hour   **Serves:** 6

The early explorers traded European cast iron for furs from American Indians.

Lamb *with* Cane Syrup & Brandy

Although this lamb dish is considered French-Caribbean in origin, today it is mostly found in Guadelupe. Many of the hotels and restaurants in that area will serve this interesting entree for Sunday brunch.

Ingredients:

3 pounds cubed lamb
1 pig's foot, split
1 ounce lime juice
1/4 cup butter
1/4 cup olive oil
1/4 cup chopped parsley
6 cloves chopped garlic
3 drops Angostura bitters
2 cups diced Bermuda onions

1 cup chopped celery
1 cup diced carrots
3 tbsps red wine vinegar
1/4 cup brandy
2 cups dry red wine
1 tbsp cane syrup
1 tsp ground pimento
salt and black pepper

Wash pig's foot well and marinate in lime juice for 30 minutes. Set aside. In a 10-quart cast iron Dutch oven, heat butter and olive oil over medium-high heat. In a large mixing bowl, combine lamb, pig's foot, parsley, garlic and bitters. Season meat well using salt and pepper. Saute the seasoned meat until golden brown on all sides. Add onions, celery and carrots. Saute 3-5 minutes or until vegetables are wilted. Add red wine vinegar, brandy, red wine and cane syrup. Blend well with the meat mixture. Bring mixture to a rolling boil and reduce to simmer. Cook, stirring occasionally, until meat is tender, approximately 2 hours. Add ground pimento and adjust seasonings if necessary.

Prep Time: 3 Hours **Serves**: 6

Stove Hollow Ware—Skillet
From a 1920s Lodge Cast Iron Catalog

41

Prune Ice Cream & Pumpkin Pancakes

Although most people think of ice cream in the summer, here in the Caribbean it's always summer. This interesting dish is found mostly in the Dutch Caribbean and originated as a Christmas dish. It is still common in many kitchens today.

Ingredients:

1 cup chopped prunes	1 1/2 cups sugar
1 cup pureed pumpkin	2 egg yolks
1 quart milk	1/4 cup brown sugar
2 cups heavy whipping cream	1/4 cup melted butter
2 cinnamon sticks	1 cup flour
2 tbsps vanilla	3/4 cup milk
8 egg yolks	1/8 tsp cinnamon powder

To make ice cream: Place 1 quart milk, whipping cream, cinnamon sticks and vanilla in a 2-quart cast iron sauce pot over medium-high heat. Simmer for 10 minutes. Remove and set aside. In a large mixing bowl combine 8 egg yolks and 1 1/2 cups sugar. Blend well until creamy and pale yellow. Ladle half of the hot milk into the egg mixture. Stir constantly to temper eggs. Add egg mixture back into the sauce pot and simmer for 2 minutes, stirring constantly. Do not boil. Remove ice cream custard from heat and discard cinnamon sticks. Chill custard over an ice bath until cool to the touch or, preferably, in the refrigerator overnight. Fold in the chopped prunes, place in a homestyle ice cream freezer and freeze according to manufacturer's directions. When done, place in freezer compartment of refrigerator for later use.

To make cakes: Combine remaining egg yolks, brown sugar and melted butter in a large mixing bowl. Using a wire whisk, blend well. Sprinkle in flour, a little at a time, until all is incorporated. Pour in remaining milk, whisking constantly, until smooth. Fold in pumpkin and cinnamon powder, blending well. When ready to serve, heat a 10-inch cast iron skillet over medium-high heat. Spray with vegetable spray or add a small amount of butter. Drop batter by tablespoons and fry until golden brown. If batter is too thin, stiffen with a small amount of flour. Serve warm pancakes with a scoop of prune ice cream.

Prep Time: 1 Hour   **Serves:** 6

A Page *from* Our Past . . .

From a 1920s Lodge Cast Iron Catalog

Chapter 4
Cajun & Creole

Like the murky bayous and rivers which have meandered through the Louisiana Delta for millions of years, the culinary gumbo now known as Cajun-Creole cuisine has been a slowly developing blend of flavors and ingredients. Contributing to this cauldron over the years were seven primary nations and cultures: the Native Americans, the French, the Spanish, the Africans, the English Americans, the Germans and the Italians. From these vital seven nations came a melting pot of flavors that are known and sought-after worldwide.

Native tribes settled in Louisiana as early as 12,000 years ago living on a diet of shellfish, alligator, bear, wild boar, deer, game birds, seeds, nuts, squash, corn and beans. They used the sassafras leaves (file powder) as a thickener in their stews and bay leaves to season. The popular dish we call maque choux is based on the Native American dish and contains corn, bell pepper, lima beans, and tomatoes.

French explorers began arriving in the first years of the 1700s, and by the time the City of New Orleans was founded in 1718, corn was a staple in the colonial diets. The kitchens of the French aristocrats produced coq au vin, etouffee, sauce piquante, pommes souffles, cassoulets, and of course, bouillabaisse, the origin of the Louisiana gumbo. The French- speaking Canadians, now known as Cajuns, fled from Nova Scotia in 1755. Their previous use of the lobster in cooking led to their creative cooking methods for the Louisiana crawfish.

The Spanish controlled the Louisiana territory from 1766 to 1803 after France turned over the territory for fear of losing it to England. The Spanish introduced the word "Creole" to identify descendants of European ancestry who kept to their homeland customs. The Spanish began to try to reproduce their local dish paella. When they could not find the necessary ingredients, substitutions produced our now famous jambalaya.

But, possibly the greatest influence on the culinary melting pot of Louisiana was the African hand. As the West African slaves began arriving in 1719, they brought with them knowledge from the sugar cane and rice plantations of the Caribbean. Gumbo, rice dishes, cooking of leafy greens, the use of beans with meat as seasoning, and the piquant (chilis of multiple varieties), were the basis of the African diet and, eventually, their European and American owners. The most pronounced contribution from Africans, however, was okra, a key ingredient in gumbo and so many other Louisiana dishes.

The English influence appeared in the area in 1804 when the "Americans" moved to the region following the Louisiana Purchase. They moved west to establish new rice, cotton and indigo plantations, and they brought with them their culinary roots and farming methods from the Virginias and Carolinas.

The largest German immigration occurred between 1850 and 1900 as the Germans began to settle along the river to establish farming, dairying and butchering operations. They became merchants, bankers and shippers in New Orleans. Our Louisiana sausages and meats, such as the andouille, tasso and boudin are evidence of the German influence.

Finally, it was around the turn of the century that the majority of Italians began to arrive. They opened groceries and restaurants and were responsible for creating some of the classic cuisine of New Orleans such as the muffaletta.

The foods we all know and love as Cajun-Creole are simply a derivation of the classical foods from these seven nations which came together to create this diverse and colorful menu. Our jambalaya, gumbo, etouffee, bisque, stew, piquante, can all be traced to these generous nations. All that we know as Louisiana cooking is a reflection of the many lands which joined to stir the cast iron pots containing Louisiana's bounty.

Chef John D. Folse

Born on Cabanocey Plantation in St. James Parish, Louisiana, Chef John Folse realized early in life that the foods and cooking styles of his culture were unique.

Cajuns, descendants of the French Acadians, fled to Louisiana after the British deported them from Acadia in Nova Scotia and the Maritime provinces of Canada in 1755. They learned to adapt their cooking by using ingredients indigenous to the area and did not try to recreate the classical cuisine of Europe.

Creoles, on the other hand, were European-born aristocrats wooed to Louisiana by the Spanish to establish New Orleans around 1690. They brought from Europe their wealth, education and cooks with a knowledge of European cooking styles. Influences from France, Spain, Germany, Italy and Africa crept into the cooking pots of these new Americans, and their cooking reflected it.

Today, Chef John Folse is recognized around the world as a leading authority on Cajun and Creole cuisine. He has two award-winning restaurants: Lafitte's Landing in Donaldsonville, Louisiana; and White Oak Plantation in Baton Rouge.

In addition to managing his two restaurants, he is host of the National PBS series "A Taste of Louisiana with Chef John Folse & Company" and his syndicated radio show "Stirrin' It Up!" He also oversees Louisiana's Premier Products, his cook and chill plant in New Orleans that manufactures soups, sauces, entrees and meats for food service and retail establishments across the country.

In 1990, Chef Folse was named National Chef of the Year by the American Culinary Federation and in 1994 was elected president of this illustrious organization. In 1992, he received an honorary doctorate of culinary arts from Johnson and Wales University, the hospitality industry's largest university, where he also served as the commencement speaker, one of the most prestigious honors of his career.

The highlight of his career came recently when Nicholls State University, Folse's alma mater in Thibodaux, Louisiana, named its new culinary program in his honor. An associate of science degree in culinary arts began this year, and a bachelor of science degree in culinary arts program is scheduled to start in 1997.

"As a chef, I cannot survive in the kitchen without my cast iron skillets. They are perfect for sauteing foods at high heat, because they don't warp under the stress of the temperatures required to create perfect finishes on delicate foods.

"The two most traditional foods of this region are jambalaya and gumbo. The only way to make an authentic roux with its intense flavors is in cast iron. If these dishes aren't made in cast iron, they aren't authentic."

Pork & Sausage Jambalaya

Jambalaya has become the best known rice dish in America. The origin of this dish cannot be disputed. When the early Spanish settlers came to New Orleans in the early 1700s, they brought with them the recipe for their famous paella. Since the ingredients for paella were not to be found in South Louisiana, their recipe was quickly adapted to the products at hand. Oysters and crawfish replaced clams and mussels in the recipe. Andouille took the place of ham and the new dish emerged from the paella pans of the Spanish. Since the main ingredient in the dish was rice, the dish was named "jambon a la yaya." "Yaya" is the African word for rice and there is no argument that the black hand in the pot had a tremendous influence in our jambalaya. Today, the dish is made with many variations and with whatever is available. The most popular combination, however, is pork, chicken and andouille.

Ingredients:

3 pounds cubed pork	8 cups beef or chicken stock
2 pounds sliced andouille	2 cups sliced mushrooms
1/4 cup Crisco or bacon drippings	1 cup sliced green onions
2 cups chopped onions	1/2 cup chopped parsley
2 cups chopped celery	salt and black pepper
1 cup chopped bell pepper	Louisiana Gold Pepper Sauce
1/2 cup diced garlic	5 cups Uncle Ben's Long Grain Rice

In a 7-quart cast iron Dutch oven, heat Crisco or bacon drippings over medium-high heat. Saute cubed pork until dark brown on all sides and some pieces are sticking to the bottom of the pot, approximately 30 minutes. This is very important as the brown color of jambalaya is derived from the color of the meat. Add andouille and saute an additional 10-15 minutes. Tilt the pot to one side and ladle out all oil, except for one large cooking spoon. Add onions, celery, bell pepper and garlic. Saute until all vegetables are well caramelized. Be careful, as vegetables will tend to scorch since the pot is so hot. Add beef stock, bring to a rolling boil and reduce heat to simmer. Cook 15 minutes for flavors to develop. Add mushrooms, green onions and parsley. Season to taste using salt, pepper and Louisiana Gold. I suggest that you slightly over-season since the rice tends to require a little extra seasoning. Add rice, reduce heat to simmer and cover. Cook rice 30-45 minutes, stirring at 20 minute intervals.

Prep Time: 2 1/2 Hours   **Serves:** 8

Fricassee of Wild Rabbit

The fricassee is probably the most popular method of cooking rabbit in South Louisiana. Slowly cooked in the cast iron pot, this simple dish is considered the best-tasting rabbit dish in Bayou country.

Ingredients:

2 young wild rabbits
3/4 cup oil
2 cups flour
2 cups chopped onions
1 cup chopped celery
1 cup chopped bell pepper

2 tbsps diced garlic
1 cup diced tomatoes
2 cups sliced oyster mushrooms
4 cups beef or chicken stock
salt and black pepper

Cut each rabbit into 8 serving pieces and season well using salt and pepper. In a 12-inch cast iron skillet, heat oil over medium-high heat. Dredge rabbit in flour, shaking off all excess. Brown well on both sides in hot oil. Once browned, remove and set aside. To the same skillet, add onions, celery, bell pepper, garlic and tomatoes. Saute until vegetables are wilted, approximately 3-5 minutes. Return rabbit to the skillet and stir well into seasonings. Add mushrooms and beef stock. Season to taste using salt and pepper. Bring the stock to a low boil, reduce heat to simmer and cover. Allow fricassee to braise for 1 1/2 hours. Rabbit will be done when it is tender to the touch. Add stock, if necessary, should mixture become too dry. Correct seasonings if necessary. The dish should be served over hot white rice with a side dish of white beans.

Prep Time: 2 Hours **Serves:** 6

Sugar Kettle
From a 1920s Lodge Cast Iron Catalog

 Iron pots and skillets were considered part of the "Crown Jewels" by Edward III in 1327.

Louisiana Seafood Gumbo

The premier soup of Cajun country, seafood gumbo is known worldwide as the dish to seek out when visiting South Louisiana. There are as many recipes for this soup as there are people who cook it. However, this is my favorite.

Ingredients:

1 pound (35 count) shrimp, peeled and deveined
1 pound jumbo lump crabmeat
2 dozen shucked oysters, reserve liquid
1 cup vegetable oil
1 cup flour
2 cups chopped onions
1 cup chopped celery
1 cup chopped bell pepper
1/4 cup diced garlic
1/2 pound sliced andouille sausage
1 pound claw crabmeat
3 quarts shellfish stock
2 cups sliced green onions
1/2 cup chopped parsley
salt and black pepper
Louisiana Gold Pepper Sauce

In a 7-quart cast iron Dutch oven, heat oil over medium-high heat. Once oil is hot, add flour and, using a wire whisk, stir constantly until brown roux is achieved. Do not allow roux to scorch. Should black specks appear in roux, discard and begin again. Once roux is golden brown, add onions, celery, bell pepper and garlic. Saute until vegetables are wilted, approximately 3-5 minutes. Add andouille, blend well into vegetable mixture and saute 2-3 minutes. Add claw crabmeat and stir into roux. This will begin to add seafood flavor to mixture. Slowly add hot shellfish stock, one ladle at a time, stirring constantly until all is incorporated. Bring to a low boil, reduce to simmer and cook approximately 30 minutes. Add additional stock if necessary to retain volume. Add green onions and parsley. Season to taste using salt, pepper and Louisiana Gold. Fold shrimp, lump crabmeat, oysters and reserved oyster liquid into soup. Return to a low boil and cook approximately 10 minutes. Adjust seasonings and serve over cooked rice.

Prep Time: 1 Hour   **Serves:** 12

Cast iron is heirloom cookware.

Louisiana Crawfish Etouffee

The French word "etouffee" means to stew, smother or braise. This technique is found in dishes using shrimp, crab, crawfish and in many cases, meat or game. Though more Creole in origin, etouffees are found throughout Cajun country.

Ingredients:

2 pounds cleaned crawfish tails
1/4 pound butter
1 cup chopped onions
1 cup chopped celery
1/2 cup chopped green
    bell pepper
1/2 cup chopped red bell pepper
1/2 cup diced tomatoes
2 tbsps diced garlic

2 bay leaves
1/2 cup tomato sauce
1 cup flour
2 quarts crawfish stock or water
1 ounce sherry
1 cup chopped green onions
1/2 cup chopped parsley
salt and black pepper
Louisiana Gold Pepper Sauce

In a 5-quart cast iron Dutch oven, melt butter over medium-high heat. Add onions, celery, bell peppers, tomatoes, garlic and bay leaves. Saute until vegetables are wilted, approximately 3-5 minutes. Add half of the crawfish tails and the tomato sauce, blending well into the mixture. Using a cooking spoon, blend flour into the vegetable mixture to form a white roux. Slowly add crawfish stock or water, a little at a time, until all is incorporated. Bring to a low boil, reduce to simmer and cook 30 minutes, stirring occasionally. Add remaining crawfish tails, sherry, green onions and parsley. Cook an additional 5 minutes. Season to taste using salt, pepper and Louisiana Gold. Served over steamed white rice.

Prep Time: 1 Hour   **Serves**: 6

Polished Hollow Ware—Dutch Oven
From a 1920s Lodge Cast Iron Catalog

 Always turn cast iron upside down in oven when seasoning.

Corn Maque Choux

Although maque choux is normally thought of as a corn soup, the Cajuns of River Road Louisiana cooked a similar vegetable flavored with the freshwater shrimp of the Mississippi River. Here is their version of that dish.

Ingredients:

8 ears fresh corn
2 cups (70-90 count) shrimp,
    peeled and deveined
1/2 cup bacon drippings
1 cup chopped onions
1/2 cup chopped celery
1/2 cup chopped green
    bell pepper

1/2 cup chopped red bell pepper
1/4 cup diced garlic
1/4 cup finely diced andouille
2 cups coarsely chopped
    tomatoes
2 tbsps tomato sauce
1 cup sliced green onions
salt and black pepper

Select tender, well-developed ears of corn and remove shucks and silk. Using a sharp knife, cut lengthwise through the kernels to remove them from the cob. Scrape each cob using the blade of the knife to remove all milk and additional pulp from the corn. This is important since the richness of the dish will depend on how much milk and pulp can be scraped from the cobs. In a 3-quart cast iron Dutch oven, melt bacon drippings over medium-high heat. Saute corn, onions, celery, bell peppers, garlic and andouille approximately 15-20 minutes or until vegetables are wilted and corn begins to tenderize. Add tomatoes, tomato sauce and shrimp. Continue cooking until juices from the tomatoes and shrimp are rendered into the dish, approximately 15-20 minutes. Add green onions and season to taste using salt and pepper. Continue to cook an additional 15 minutes or until full flavors of corn and shrimp are developed in the dish. Serve as a vegetable or add stock to create a soup.

Prep Time: 1 Hour **Serves:** 8

Wash cast iron immediately after use, while it is still hot.

Peach Cobbler

One of Louisiana's loveliest plantations, Houmas House, had many visitors back in the mid-1800s. Often they would write of their experiences at the plantation. One such visitor wrote about the wonderful peas that were grown in the garden and eaten day after day. He mentioned the mint juleps served before breakfast and the fabulous peach cobbler that ended every meal. Here is a rendition of that dish.

Ingredients:

6 cups sliced fresh peaches	pinch of nutmeg
1 1/2 cups sugar	pinch of allspice
1/4 cup water	1 cup all purpose flour
3 tbsps flour	1/2 cup sugar
1/4 cup sugar	2 tsps baking powder
pinch of salt	3/4 cup milk
pinch of cinnamon	1/2 tsp salt

Preheat oven to 400 degrees F. In a 10-inch cast iron skillet, combine peaches, 1 1/2 cups of sugar and water. Bring to a rolling boil, reduce to simmer and allow fruit to cook until softened. In a measuring cup, blend 3 tablespoons flour, 1/4 cup of sugar, salt, cinnamon, nutmeg and allspice. Pour into the peach mixture, stirring constantly until mixture thickens. Remove from heat and pour the mixture into a 12-inch cast iron skillet or cobbler pan and set aside to cool slightly. In a mixing bowl, combine remaining flour, sugar, baking powder and milk. Using a wire whisk, whip until well blended. Season with salt. Pour the batter, in an irregular shape, over the center of the cobbler. Bake for approximately 45 minutes or until golden brown. NOTE: You may wish to garnish the cobbler with fresh sliced peaches, powdered sugar and a sprig of mint.

Prep Time: 1 1/2 Hours   **Serves**: 8

 Cast Iron turns black with age.

Cracklin' Biscuits

The Cajuns, always looking for variation in recipes, certainly created a winner here. Adding the hog cracklin' to the biscuit mixture created a unique breakfast item. If you don't have cracklin's, you may wish to substitute salted pork skins.

Ingredients:

4 cups all purpose flour
2 tbsps baking powder
1 tsp baking soda
1 1/2 tbsps sugar
1 tsp salt

2/3 cup unsalted butter
1 1/2 cups buttermilk
3/4 cup chopped hog cracklin's
1/4 cup melted butter

Preheat oven to 400 degrees F. In a large mixing bowl, combine flour, baking powder, baking soda, sugar and salt. Mix well to ensure proper blending. Using a pastry blender, cut 2/3 cup of butter into flour mixture. Once butter has been well blended into flour, add buttermilk and chopped cracklin's. Continue to mix until biscuit dough is well formed. Place dough on a floured board and knead lightly. Roll dough out until approximately 3/4-inch thick. Cut biscuits with a 3-inch biscuit cutter until all are formed. Place biscuits in a greased 12-inch cast iron skillet and drizzle with remaining melted butter. Bake until golden brown, approximately 25 minutes.

Prep Time: 30 Minutes   **Makes:** 8-10 Biscuits

Stove Hollow Ware—Tea Kettle
From a 1920s Lodge Cast Iron Catalog

*Good cooks claim. "The heavier the metal . . .
the lighter the bread."*

53

Chapter 5
The Southwest

The rapid spread of Southwestern culinary cuisine is evident on menus around the nation. This phenomenon appears to stem from a variety of reasons including the flavor appeal of the cuisine's deep spice characteristics and health perceptions from salsas and glazes replacing heavily oiled dressings and butter-rich sauces.

Most research identifies the Southwest region of the United States as inclusive of the states of Texas, New Mexico and Arizona, with some including the state of Oklahoma. This set of states capture the heart of Southwest cuisine.

The Southwest Indians, particularly the Navaho and the Apache, occupied Southwest America long before the first white settlers appeared to claim the land. The abundance of indigenous game, fruits and vegetables gave these early settlers a wide pantry from which to choose. They gathered blueberries, milkweed blossoms, maize, pumpkins, cattail sap, wild rice, wild gooseberries and sweet potatoes, and they ate the berries and fruits of nearly 300 different plants.

The Spaniards were the first white men to explore and colonize the Southwest in their search for gold and silver. The Mexicans followed bringing with them quesadillas, tortillas, salsas and much more.

The states that now comprise this "Great American Desert" were settled between 1682 and 1890. However, it was not until the "cowboy era" of 1865 to 1890 that cattle drives on the open range from west Texas to Missouri allowed for the Longhorn cattle of the prairies to be transported to eastern markets. While on these drives, the cowboys dined on chuckwagon cuisine such as roasted meats basted with a concoction of bacon fat, vinegar, molasses, salt and chili peppers — a recipe that may explain the Texan passion for bar-b-que. [An entire chapter of this book is dedicated to the chuckwagon cuisine of this era]. The evolution of the refrigerated railroad cars, which began to crisscross the country in the late 1800s, diminished the need for these long trail drives and supplied

Americans with the fresh beef and pork indigenous to the Southwest. The infiltration of Chinese laborers during this time also encouraged experimentation in Mexican and Spanish cooking and led to an astonishing melting pot in the West.

Ingredients used in the preparation of this spicy and healthful Southwest cooking vary widely. Some of the best known are small, red and green hot chili peppers, cilantro, garlic, corn meal, tropical fruits and vegetables including cherries, corn, grapefruit, papaya, mangos and, of course, the avocado. The rich and abundant wildlife of the region includes bears, deer, jackrabbits, sheep, elk, antelope, quail and duck.

Chefs are creating wonderful masterpieces from this array of ingredients. Typical dishes include smoked-corn cilantro gazpacho, black beans, chicken burritos, tomato tortilla soup with smoked chicken and fried tortilla strips, Southwest crab cakes with ancho cilantro crema, mesquite grilled chicken with roasted corn and jicama relish and home fried potatoes topped with chorizo, hot peppers and Montercy Jack cheese. In the Southwest a simple steak is turned into a culinary masterpiece with the addition of a spicy chile pepper sauce, and roasted peppers and garlic give a new twist to wild game and meats of the region.

When venturing to the Southwest, or just trying your hand at one of the great Southwestern recipes included in this book, be prepared for a realm of spice and flavor that will provide a tantalizing adventure for your tastebuds.

Chef Maurice Zeck

Chef Maurice Zeck has spent a lifetime honing his skills as an award winning Southwestern chef. As a result of his efforts, he was selected as the winner of the prestigious Western Regional Chef of the

Year Award by the American Culinary Federation in 1994.

In addition, he is a world-class ice carver. His honors range from preparing ice sculptures at million-dollar fund raisers in Las Vegas to carving artistic pieces that have graced the plaza at Taos during Christmas.

As the executive chef at the La Fonda Hotel, one of the West's oldest hotels, Chef Zeck places a great emphasis on preparing specialties appropriate for this adobe-style historic inn located at the end of the Santa Fe Trail.

It is here that he prepares what he considers to be historically true dishes born of the unique marriage of Spanish, Mexican, Neo-Continental and American cuisines. Chili dishes and Southwest cooking originated here, and Chef Zeck enjoys recreating these specialties from the hub of the melting pot of these cultures.

To Chef Zeck, these foods are a unique blend of cultures and cuisines. The braised meats, deep dish stews and corn tortillas are best prepared in cast iron for a rich flavor and desired consistency. "I consider my craft to be a marriage of ingredients and concept. By using traditional preparation techniques, traditional foods and ingredients and cast iron, which is traditional American cookware, I am creating truly traditional foods."

Cactus Pan
From a current Lodge Cast Iron Catalog

Venison Shanks *with* Corn Meal Cakes

As hunters, we have an obligation to utilize all of the animal that we harvest. This seldom used cut is the tastiest of all.

Ingredients:

6 (6-8 ounce) venison shanks
1/2 cup vegetable oil
1 1/2 cups all purpose flour
2 cups red wine
1 quart game stock or beef stock
1/2 cup diced garlic
6 sprigs fresh thyme

2 ounces salt pork
1/2 cup diced turnips
1/2 diced rutabagas
1/4 cup pearl onions, peeled
12 fresh or dried Morel
mushrooms

Season shanks well using salt and pepper. In a 10-quart cast iron Dutch oven, heat vegetable oil over medium-high heat. Dust shanks in flour, shaking off excess. Sear shanks on all sides until golden brown. Remove and keep warm. In the same pot, sprinkle in 3/4 cup remaining flour. Using a wire whisk, whip until light brown roux is achieved. Add red wine and game stock, blending well into the roux mixture. Additional stock may be necessary to achieve sauce-like consistency. Bring mixture to a rolling boil and reduce to simmer. Return shanks to sauce then add garlic, thyme and salt pork. Cover and simmer for 1 1/2 - 2 hours or until shanks are fork-tender but not falling apart. Preheat oven to 350 degrees F. When shanks are tender, remove from pot, place on a cookie sheet and keep warm. Add all remaining vegetables directly into the sauce. Cover and bake for 1 hour or until vegetables are al dente. Return the shanks to the pot and reheat 15-20 minutes. Serve shanks, surrounded by vegetables and a portion of corn meal cakes.

For Corn Meal Cakes:

1 1/2 cups yellow corn meal
3 cups chicken stock
1/4 cup butter
1/2 cup sliced green onions

1/2 cup diced red bell pepper
1 tsp salt
2 tsps cracked black pepper
1/2 cup butter

In a 5-quart cast iron Dutch oven, place stock and butter over medium-high heat. Bring mixture to a rolling boil and reduce heat to simmer. Slowly add corn meal. Using a wire whisk, stir constantly until corn meal absorbs the liquid and starts to pull away from the sides of the pot. Add green onions and red bell pepper. Season to taste using salt and pepper. Remove the corn meal to a large mixing bowl and allow to cool slightly. Form corn meal into twelve 3-inch patties. In a 10-inch cast iron skillet, melt 1/2 cup butter over medium-high heat. Saute corn meal cakes until golden brown on each side. Serve warm with venison shanks.

Prep Time: 30 minutes   **Serves:** 6

Classic Relleno *with* Cilantro Coulis

This is the original LaFonda recipe that dates back to 1925. It still works for thousands of guests each year. If its not broken, don't fix it!

Ingredients:

6 whole green chiles, roasted
   and peeled
3/4 cup fresh goat cheese
3/4 cup cheddar cheese

1 cup lard
1/2 cup all purpose flour
4 eggs, beaten

In a food processor fitted with a metal blade, place goat and cheddar cheeses. Beat until smooth and creamy. Remove and place in a pastry bag with a #5 round tip. Set aside. Using a paring knife, cut a 1-inch slice at the stem end of each green chile. Fill each chile with cheese mixture. In a 12-inch cast iron skillet, melt lard over medium-high heat. Dip chile in flour, shaking off all excess and then in egg. Dust again in flour and deep fry until golden brown on all sides. Remove and drain on paper towels. To serve, place hot relleno on a generous portion of cilantro coulis.

Ingredients:

6 red chiles, roasted and peeled
1/2 bunch cilantro, chopped
1/2 cup shallots, minced

1 cup hot chicken stock
1 tsp salt
1 tsp white pepper

Place all ingredients in a food processor fitted with a metal blade. Puree until smooth. Ladle one ounce of warm coulis in the center of a 8-inch appetizer plate. Top with classic relleno.

Prep Time: 45 Minutes   **Serves:** 6

58

Fire-Roasted Corn Chowder

This recipe came from the fire-roasted chile technique. Corn and chile are still fire-roasted throughout New Mexico.

Ingredients:

4 ears of corn
1 ounce salt pork, ground
1/2 cup diced green bell pepper
1/2 cup diced red bell pepper
1/2 cup diced yellow bell pepper
1/2 cup diced Spanish onion
1/2 cup flour

4 cups chicken stock
4 large potatoes, quartered
1 tbsp red chile powder
1 tsp cumin
1 tsp chile pequin
1 tsp salt
1 tsp white pepper

Preheat barbecue grill according to manufacturer's directions. Place corn on the grill and roast over mesquite coals until grilled and smokey flavor is achieved, approximately 10-15 minutes. Remove corn and, using a sharp paring knife, cut corn from the cob. With the back of the knife blade, scrape the cob well to remove the sweet cream. Add cream to kernels and set aside. In a 7-quart cast iron Dutch oven, saute salt pork until juices are rendered. Add bell peppers and onions. Saute until vegetables are wilted, approximately 3-5 minutes. Sprinkle in flour and, using a wire whisk, stir constantly until light roux is achieved. Slowly add chicken stock, one ladle at a time, until all is incorporated. Add corn, potatoes, chile powder and cumin. Bring mixture to a rolling boil and reduce heat to simmer. Allow chowder to simmer for 10 minutes. Add chile pequin, salt and pepper. Additional stock may be necessary to retain soup-like consistency. Serve warm with garlic croutons. **Prep Time:** 1 Hour **Serves:** 6

Cast iron Dutch oven is the original slow cooker.

Calabasa Skillet Souffle

This is an Old Mexico recipe brought to LaFonda by Guadalupe Rodriguez from her mother's kitchen in Chichuahu, Mexico.

Ingredients:

1/2 cup vegetable oil
1/2 cup diced chayote squash
1/2 cup diced summer squash
1/2 cup diced zucchini
1/2 cup diced onion
1/2 cup whole kernel corn

7 egg yolks
2 1/2 cups heavy whipping
   cream
1 tsp salt
1 tsp white pepper

Preheat oven to 350 degrees F. In a 12-inch cast iron skillet, heat oil over medium-high heat. Add squash, onions and corn. Saute until vegetables are wilted, approximately 10 minutes. In a mixing bowl, combine egg yolks and cream. Remove skillet from heat and pour egg mixture into the vegetables, blending thoroughly. Season to taste using salt and pepper. Cover the skillet and bake in oven until souffle is set, approximately 30 minutes. Remove from heat and let rest for 10 minutes. Serve warm.

Prep Time: 1 Hour   **Serves:** 6

Indoor/Outdoor Combo Cooker
From a current Lodge Cast Iron Catalog

Cooking foods with fat content expedites seasoning cast iron.

Sage Flatbread

A new LaFonda tradition.

Ingredients:

2 cups warm water
1 tbsp yeast
1 tbsp sugar
1/2 tsp paprika
1 tbsp garlic powder

2 tbsps dried sage
1/2 cup extra virgin olive oil
1 tbsp salt
3 cups all purpose flour

Grease a 5-quart cast iron Dutch oven. Preheat oven to 350 degrees F. In the bowl of an electric mixer fitted with a dough hook, place water, yeast and sugar. Beat on low speed until ingredients are thoroughly blended. Let rest 5 minutes. Add spices, oil and salt. Add flour, a little at a time, mixing constantly on low speed until all is incorporated. Mix a total of 10 minutes. Turn out dough onto a floured surface and fold into itself four times. NOTE: Do not add any flour as dough should be soft. Place dough in Dutch oven and press flat with your fingers. Cover with a towel and allow dough to rise approximately double in volume, then press down with your fingers once again. Cover with towel and repeat the rising process. Bake for 30 minutes or until golden brown. **Prep Time:** 2 Hours **Serves:** 6

Campfire Biscuit Cobbler

New Mexico is still a ranchers paradise. One of the few "open-range" states left in our country — the old tradition runs strong.

Ingredients:

1/4 cup corn starch
1/2 cup water
3 cups water
3/4 cup Jack Daniels whiskey
3/4 cup brown sugar
1/2 tbsp cinnamon

1/2 tsp nutmeg
1 1/2 cups apples,
  peeled and diced
1 1/2 cups rhubarb, diced
1 1/2 cups sweet potatoes, peeled

Preheat oven to 375 degrees F. In a large mixing bowl, place corn starch and 1/2 cup water. Using a wire whisk, blend ingredients thoroughly. Set aside. In a 3-quart cast iron Dutch oven, place 3

cups water, Jack Daniels, brown sugar, cinnamon and nutmeg.
Bring mixture to a rolling boil and reduce heat to simmer. In
separate batches, blanch apples, rhubarb and sweet potatoes in
syrup until tender. When fruit is tender, remove and drain. Bring
liquid back to a rolling boil. Blend corn starch thoroughly and,
using a wire whisk, add to the simmering liquid until thickened.
Remove from heat and add poached fruit. Transfer mixture to a 12-
inch cast iron skillet and cool slightly. Cover fruit with biscuit
topping and bake 25-30 minutes or until golden brown. Serve
warm with your favorite ice cream.

Ingredients for Biscuit Topping:

4 cups all purpose flour

1 1/2 cups shortening

1/2 cup sugar

1 tbsp salt

1/4 cup baking powder

3/4 cup buttermilk

3 whole eggs

In a small mixing bowl, sift all dry ingredients together. Cut in
shortening and set aside. In another small mixing bowl, combine
buttermilk and eggs. Pour buttermilk mixture into shortening
mixture and combine. Do not overmix. Form biscuit dough into a
circle approximately 1/2-inch thick and large enough to cover the
fruit. Place dough over fruit mixture in the skillet prior to baking.
Bake for 25-30 minutes or until golden brown. Serve warm.

Prep Time: 1 Hour   **Serves:** 6

Stove Hollow Ware—Sad Iron Heater
From a 1920s Lodge Cast Iron Catalog

 Season cast iron inside and out, including lids.

A Page *from* Our Past . . .

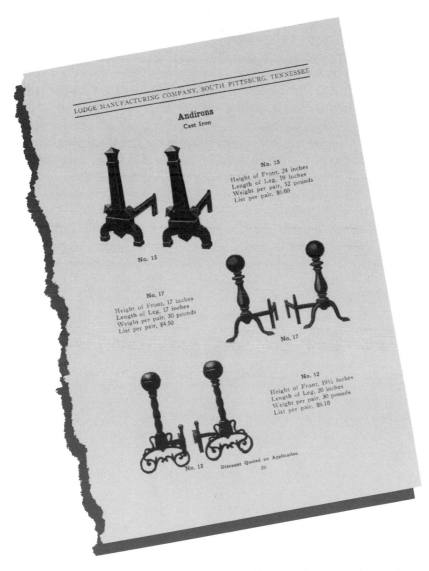

LODGE MANUFACTURING COMPANY, SOUTH PITTSBURG, TENNESSEE

Andirons
Cast Iron

No. 15
Height of Front, 24 inches
Length of Leg, 19 inches
Weight per pair, 52 pounds
List per pair, $6.00

No. 15

No. 17
Height of Front, 17 inches
Length of Leg, 17 inches
Weight per pair, 30 pounds
List per pair, $4.50

No. 17

No. 12
Height of Front, 19½ inches
Length of Leg, 20 inches
Weight per pair, 30 pounds
List per pair, $6.10

No. 12   Discount Quoted on Application
20

From a 1920s Lodge Cast Iron Catalog

Chapter 6
Chuck Wagon

Even though the height of the "cowboy era" lasted a mere 25 years, from 1865 to 1890, the cowboy is as recognized a symbol in the United States today as the bald eagle or the Stars and Stripes.

West Texas was the origin point of the era when ranchers returning from the Civil War found millions of head of Longhorn cattle roaming the prairies unattended and unclaimed. Before the era ended, the cowboys had expanded as far west as Montana and as far north as the Dakotas.

The cattle drive phenomenon started as ranchers began to learn of the hunger for beef in the northern and eastern regions. This translated to an opportunity to make the West productive again. The cowboys, Mexicans, Blacks, and frontiersmen of varied cultural backgrounds, melded into cohesive teams and moved herds of 1,200 to 3,000 head to Missouri railheads 1,000 miles away for shipment to the eastern markets.

In 1866, Charles Goodnight invented an addition to these long cattle drives which made life on the open range much more tolerable — the chuck wagon. This farm wagon, which was converted into a mobile kitchen, was a welcomed luxury. The first wagons contained a large water barrel, a toolbox, a canopy frame for protection, and most important, the chuck box. Beneath the chuck box was storage for the cook's utensils, and a calfskin hammock suspended under the wagon carried a collection of firewood and "prairie coal."

Because he needed to feed a crew of men with foods that would last several months in the scorching heat, the chuck wagon cook used dry supplies such as coffee, beans, baking powder, flour, corn meal, rice, sugar, dried chili peppers, dried fruit, salt pork and canned foods. With these ingredients the chuck wagon cooks had to be able to build and cook over an open fire. Hardwood was used for fuel and mesquite for flavor.

For his crew, the cook would prepare the favorites such as simple soups and stews, sourdough biscuits and breads, and the most popular dish, chili. For vegetables, the cowboys liked onions and potatoes. Contrary to popular belief, beef was not a regular staple in the diet of cowboys since it was not economical to kill the ranchers product and also since, without refrigeration, the leftovers were sure to spoil. Instead, fresh meat was usually rabbit, antelope, deer or prairie grouse. These meats were basted with a concoction of bacon fat, vinegar, molasses, salt and chili peppers — the start of the Texas passion for bar-b-que.

With the expansion of the railroad and the invention of barbed wire in the 1890s, the need for long trail drives diminished and the cowboy, along with his chuck wagon, quickly became a part of history. The cowboy became the symbol of the frontier spirit of courage, independence and self-reliance. The chuck wagon cooks, with their ingenuity and adaptive nature, created a special cuisine from the basic foods of meat, beans and bread. This cuisine is still an integral part of the Southwest culture today.

Chef Jim Anderson

Chef Jim Anderson began his career in chuck wagon cooking by learning about one of its most basic components—beef! After earning a Master of Science Degree in Meat Science from Oklahoma State University and a Bachelor of Science degree from Oklahoma A&M's College of Agriculture, he gained additional experience in restaurants, food companies and hospitality chains for more than 30 years.

Today he is Assistant Professor and Business Manager for the School of Hotel and Restaurant Administration at Oklahoma State in Stillwater. In addition, he is certified as a Foodservice Management Professional by the National Restaurant Association and is a member of the Oklahoma Restaurant Association. He also owns the Garfield County Grill, a restaurant and catering operation in Enid, Oklahoma.

Chef Anderson has also authored articles and books about the restaurant business. He authored a chapter of *Restaurant Biz is Show Biz* and wrote *Blueprint for a Restaurant Turn-Around*.

Chef Anderson considers his chuck wagon cooking experiences as the fun parts of his career. He discovered his interest in it while exploring his roots more than 20 years ago. Both his grandfathers drove cattle and horses along the Chisholm Trail from San Antonio to Kansas, and they were seasoned cowboys who knew how to survive rough winters by cooking hearty meals in the only cookware they had—cast iron Dutch ovens.

His interest has continued through the years, and about three years ago, Jim joined the Cherokee Strip Chuck wagon Association for those who enjoy this type of cooking and want to keep its history alive. Once a year, they spend a week on an authentic cattle drive, living and cooking like they did on the old Chisholm Trail. And now, like then, the best way to cook is still in a cast iron Dutch oven.

"Everything about our cattle drives is as close to the old days as we can get, especially our food and the way we cook it. Like those cowboys, we rely on our Dutch ovens to prepare those delicious hearty meals. Dutch oven cooking is a great hobby that's taught me a lot about the food of old days."

Chisholm Trail
Corn-*on-the*-Cob

After a day in the saddle, cowboys are ready to eat! Chuck wagon cooks could hold off those starving cowboys with a few fresh ears of sweet corn while they prepared the evening chow. This same simple idea can work for your backyard barbeque as an appetizer.

Ingredients:

12 ears of sweet corn, shuck-on   1 tsp salt
1/2 pound butter   1 tsp pepper

Place a 12-quart cast iron dutch oven over medium-high heat. Place corn in pot and cover with cold water. Bring water to a rolling boil and cook 25 minutes. Remove corn from water and, using rubber gloves, peel down the husk without removing it. The husk now forms the handle which makes it convenient to serve. Remove the corn silk, then brush corn with butter. Season to taste using salt and pepper. Serve warm.

Prep Time: 1 Hour   **Serves**: 6

Stove Hollow Ware — Long Griddle
From a 1920s Lodge Cast Iron Catalog

Cast iron is the original waterless cookware.

Chisholm Trail Spoon Steak Chili

Chisholm Trail cowboys referred to a great bowl of chili as "spoon steak," while Texans called it a "bowl of red." Some say chili con carne had its start in Texas in the early 1800s. Frank Talbut's Bowl of Red *book ends with this prayer: "Chili eaters is some of YOUR chosen people. We don't know why YOU so doggone good to us. But Lord, God, don't think we ain't grateful for this chili we about to eat. Amen."*

Ingredients:

2 pounds ground beef
1 large onion, chopped
3/4 tsps flour
1 quart tomato juice
1 package chili seasoning

2 tsps chili powder
1/2 cup ketchup
3 cans chili beans
2 cans beef consomme

In a 5-quart cast iron Dutch oven, place ground beef over medium-high heat. Saute until meat is brown and separated grain for grain, approximately 30 minutes. Add onion and saute 10 additional minutes. Sprinkle in flour and blend well into the meat mixture. Add tomato juice, chili seasonings, ketchup, beans and consomme. Bring mixture to a rolling boil and reduce heat to simmer. Allow chili to cook a minimum of 1 hour, stirring occasionally. You may wish to adjust seasonings using a pinch of salt and pepper. Serve warm.

Prep Time: 2 Hours   **Serves:** 6

Recipe from: Marsh Green - Jefferson Ranch Team

 Cast iron must be preheated slowly and evenly to prevent stress breaks.

Chisholm Trail
Fried Prairie Oysters

The only "seafood" the cook could find along the Chisholm Trail was the "prairie oyster." During the roundups, when the cowboys made young bulls into steers, the harvested testicles were fried for a great treat at the end of the day. For the city slickers, serve with cocktail sauce.

Ingredients:

12 prairie oysters (calf fries)
1/2 cup flour
1 cup vegetable oil
1/4 cup milk

2 cups cracker crumbs
1 tsp salt
1 tsp black pepper

Frozen calf fries should be slit lengthwise and tips cut off. Peel fries and cut into 1/2-inch slices and rinse under cold running water. Season flour to taste using salt and pepper. In a 12-inch cast iron skillet, heat oil over medium-high heat. Dampen calf fries in milk, then press into cracker crumbs. Pan fry in skillet until golden brown and crispy.

Prep Time: 30 Minutes   **Serves:** 6

Recipe from: Dick Autry - Garber Ranch Team

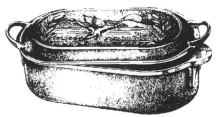

Sportsman's Cooker
From a current Lodge Cast Iron Catalog

Chisholm Trail Parsleyed Sour Cream Potatoes

Fresh vegetables along the Chisholm Trail were a rare treat. The only perishables stocked on a chuck wagon were potatoes and onions. This simple potato recipe turns out great every time and can be prepared easily, even by inexperienced cooks.

Ingredients:

12 large potatoes
1/4 cup dried parsley
2 pints sour cream
1 pound bacon, cut into pieces
1 cup sliced green onions

1 cup half and half
1 cup grated cheddar cheese
1 tsp salt
1 tsp pepper

Peel potatoes and cut into 1-inch pieces. In a 5-quart cast iron Dutch oven, place potatoes with enough water to cover by 1 inch. Bring water to a rolling boil over medium-high heat and cook until tender. Do not overcook. Drain and cool potatoes. In the same Dutch oven, place bacon. Fry until golden brown and crispy. Remove bacon and reserve 1 tablespoon of bacon fat in the Dutch oven. Set bacon aside for later use. Return potatoes to Dutch oven and place over medium heat. Coat well with bacon fat and add parsley, sour cream, green onions and half and half. Season mixture to taste using salt and pepper. Allow mixture to cook approximately 15-20 minutes, stirring occasionally. Remove from heat. Sprinkle in cheese and bacon and stir gently until cheese is melted. Serve hot.

Prep Time: 1 Hour   **Serves:** 10-12

Stove Hollow Ware—Bulged Pot
From a 1920s Lodge Cast Iron Catalog

Chisholm Trail Southwest Swiss Steak

All cowboys and cowgirls like beef and this recipe is prepared from the less expensive cuts of round steak. The secret of turning this cheaper cut into a great tasting meal is the pounding of the flour-seasoning mixture into the meat which also tenderizes it. This recipe has won several prizes at dutch oven cookoffs.

Ingredients:

3 pounds boneless round steak, cut into serving pieces
3/4 cup flour
2 tsps salt
2 tsps black pepper
1/2 tsp garlic salt
3 tbsps vegetable oil
1 cup chopped onions
1/2 cup chopped celery
1/2 cup chopped green bell pepper
1/4 cup diced garlic
1 (28-ounce) can diced tomatoes
1 cup beef broth
1 tbsp soy sauce
1/4 cup cold water
2 tbsps flour

In a large mixing bowl, combine 3/4 cup flour, salt, pepper and garlic salt. Using a meat mallet, pound the round steak until tender. Dredge steak in seasoned flour and continue to pound the meat lightly until the seasoned flour mixture is embedded into the grain. In a 14-inch cast iron skillet, heat oil over medium-high heat. Saute steak until golden brown on both sides. Add onions, celery, bell pepper and garlic. Saute until vegetables are wilted, approximately 3-5 minutes. Add tomatoes, broth and soy sauce. Bring mixture to a rolling boil, reduce heat to simmer and cover. Cook for 1 1/2 hours or until meat is tender. In a measuring cup, combine water and 2 tablespoons flour until flour is thoroughly dissolved. Pour flour mixture into the meat sauce until thickened. Adjust seasonings if necessary.

Prep Time: 2 Hours   **Serves:** 10-12

Never scour or put cast iron in a dishwasher.

Chisholm Trail Blueberry French Toast Cobbler

Fresh fruit was not available on the Chisholm Trail so cooks made use of sun-dried fruits whenever possible. Today, ranch teams are often lucky enough to stumble upon fresh berries in season and use these over their fresh cobblers and desserts.

Ingredients:

4 1/2 cups blueberries
1 loaf French bread, sliced
   3/4-inch thick
5 eggs
1/4 cup sugar
1/4 tsp baking powder
1 tsp vanilla

3/4 cup milk
1 tbsp butter
1/2 cup sugar
1 tsp cinnamon
1 tsp corn starch
powdered sugar

Preheat oven to 450 degrees F. Place bread in a 14-inch cast iron skillet. In a large mixing bowl, combine eggs, 1/4 cup sugar, baking powder and vanilla. Using a wire whisk, blend all ingredients thoroughly. Slowly add the milk until all is incorporated. Pour egg mixture over the bread, turning once to coat evenly. Cover and allow to set for 1 hour at room temperature. In a 5-quart cast iron Dutch oven, melt 1 tablespoon of butter over medium-high heat. In a large mixing bowl, combine 4 1/2 cups blueberries, 1/2 cup sugar, 1 teaspoon cinnamon and 1 teaspoon corn starch. Pour blueberry mixture into Dutch oven. Place bread, wettest side up, on top of blueberries. Bake for 25 minutes or until blueberries are bubbling around bread and the bread is golden brown. Remove cobbler from oven. Sprinkle powdered sugar over toast. Top with additional fresh blueberries and serve warm.

Prep Time: 45 Minutes   **Serves:** 8

 Re-season iron pots after cooking beans of any kind.

A Page *from* Our Past . . .

EODG MANUFACTURING COMPANY, SOUTH PITTSBURG, TENNESSEE

Polished Hollow Ware

Straight Kettle, Flat Bottom

No.	Diameter Top in inches	Depth in inches	Average number in Bbl.	Average weight per Bbl.	List Each Standard Finish
7	9½	6	15	140	$1.62
8	9¾	6½	12	130	1.75
9	10⅛	7⅛	9	130	2.12

Add 20% to above prices for list on Flat Bottom Bulged Pots.

Bowls, Scotch and Yankee

No.	List Each Standard Finish Scotch Bowl	List Each Standard Finish Yankee Bowl
2	$1.00	$1.12
3	1.13	1.38
4	1.25	1.62
5	1.56	1.88
6	1.75	2.25

Discount Quoted on Application

12

From a 1920s Lodge Cast Iron Catalog

Chapter 7
Pacific Northwest

Mountains and beaches come to mind when we think of the Pacific Northwest. However, there is more to this region than its breathtaking landscapes. Its rich history of discovery by the Spanish is the start of its present day story.

The Pacific Northwest is inclusive of Oregon, Washington and California. While grouped into a region, the states remain very different from one another. Although Oregon and Washington are not blessed with the sub-tropical climate and landscape of California, one which is ideal for the production of fruits and vegetables, their mountainous ranges and bountiful rivers provide an abundance of ingredients. After all, California harvests enough fruits and vegetables to easily supply its neighboring states.

As early as the 1540s, Spanish explorers on an expedition with Barlolove Verrello first spotted what we know today as Oregon. After the Spanish discovery, many other ethnic groups began to move into the Northwestern territory. Among them were Japanese, Chinese, Mexicans and immigrants transplanted from other parts of North America. Some were looking to escape the weather patterns of the midwest, others seeking work, and yet others just in search of a new land. These were certainly not the first humans to inhabit the land, however, archaeological remains point to life in the region for over 10,000 years.

From the California groves and farms come the bountiful supply of fruits and vegetables such as avocados, shallots, lettuce, tomatoes, lemons, oranges, and grapes. Apples and pears are also abundantly available from the Northwest region.

The Columbia River of Oregon serves as an important piece of the settling puzzle of the Pacific Northwest. It is home to a vast supply of the most sought-after export of the region — the Chinook salmon. The river also supplies a great variety of oysters and clams including Littleneck, Horseneck and Cockel. The smelt and rainbow trout, a well-known eating fish, and many other fish species, also call this river home.

The Great Rocky Mountains have long provided another

food source for the inhabitants of this region. Home to a large variety of deer, sheep, elk and game birds, the mountains remain today an excellent source of culinary delights. Although duck and geese remain popular, the bird of choice is by far the pheasant, which was brought to the region by the Chinese looking for a new life.

Dishes which typify the Pacific Northwest cuisine include smoked salmon, plank salmon, grilled or smoked black cod and trout, Carpet-bag Steak (steak stuffed with oysters), crab cakes, russet potatoes with rosemary, clam chowder, spiced smelt, and sauces and cobblers made from local berries.

The people of the Pacific Northwest have adapted to climates which differ greatly throughout the region and have contributed greatly to the menus of our nation.

Chef Alfred Popp

Chef Alfred Popp was born in Austria and discovered his natural talent for and interest in cooking there. In the European tradition, he began with a three-year apprenticeship in Salzburg and then began working with a series of master chefs around the world to gain exposure and develop a style of his own.

In Europe, it is believed that a chef is best trained by working short stints under different masters, and Popp gained respect as he studied in Switzerland, Hong Kong, Saudi Arabia and the Philippines.

After many years of experience, he immigrated to the United States in 1985 and joined the Marriott Corporation, gaining experience at the Twin Bridges Restaurant in Washington, D.C., and the New Orleans Marriott. He was also instrumental in the successful opening of the Marriott in Oklahoma City, Oklahoma, and was later selected as the executive chef at the Marriott in Tulsa, Oklahoma.

Today, Chef Popp owns his own catering company, A Thyme for All Seasons, in Portland, Oregon. He specializes in upscale events in private homes—ranging from intimate dinners for four to elaborate receptions for 200 or more guests.

In his spare time, Chef Popp is the president of the Southwest Washington chapter of the American Culinary Federation. He also has a keen interest in wines from the Pacific Northwest and enjoys experimenting with fresh herbs from his garden.

A specialist in the preparation of food from the Pacific Northwest, Chef Popp enjoys the readily available selections of fresh seafood, produce and regional game. In addition, the area is the largest mushroom producer in the United States.

According to Chef Popp, the Pacific Northwest offers these treats all year long at reasonable prices while chefs in other parts of the country are paying higher prices for lesser quality foods.

Traditional cuisine in the area has been influenced not only by the native Americans who settled in the area but also by the influx of immigrants to the region. The result is a great variety of foods prepared according to the eclectic backgrounds of its citizens.

Therefore, Chef Popp's appreciation of foods is focused not as much on how they are prepared but their availability and quality.

"I prepare my specialty crab cakes in a custom-made, five-foot cast iron skillet. It's not only the perfect vessel, it is a great conversation piece. I also enjoy serving individual cobblers made with fresh berries, prepared and served in small, individual-sized skillets. They are wonderful crowd pleasers—both for their taste and the presentation."

Pacific Seafood Chowder

Looking for a hearty chowder — try combining the best seafood the Pacific Northwest has to offer! Fresh mushrooms are a nice touch to this dish. Try using chanterelles, morels or chicken of the woods.

Ingredients:

8 ounces cooked clams, chopped
8 ounces shucked oysters,
    reserve juice
8 ounces mussels in shell
8 ounces salmon fillets, deboned
    and cut into 1-inch cubes
8 ounces halibut fillets, deboned
    and cut into 1-inch cubes
1/4 cup unsalted butter
2 medium onions, diced
1/2 cup celery, diced

1 cup carrots, diced
1 cup potatoes, diced
1 cup wild mushrooms, sliced
1 cup white wine
4 cups clam juice
1 sprig fresh thyme
2 tbsps Italian parsley, chopped
salt and black pepper
1 cup heavy whipping cream

In a 10-quart cast iron Dutch oven, melt butter over medium-high heat. Add onions, celery, carrots, potatoes and mushrooms. Saute until vegetables are wilted, approximately 3-5 minutes. Add white wine, clam juice, oyster juice, thyme and parsley. Bring mixture to a rolling boil and reduce heat to simmer. Add all of the seafood, blending well into the mixture. Cook for an additional 15 minutes or until seafood begins to fall apart. Season to taste using salt and pepper. Add heavy whipping cream and continue to simmer for 5 minutes. Ladle chowder into soup bowls and serve hot.

Prep Time: 30 Minutes   **Serves:** 6-8

Never let cast iron drip dry.

Dungeness Crab Cakes

Locals from the Washington and Oregon coasts look forward to the Dungeness crab season each year. Dungeness crab — one of the world's best shellfish — makes an excellent appetizer to accompany almost any meal.

Ingredients:

2 pounds Dungeness crabmeat, chopped
2 cups fresh bread crumbs
1/4 cup sliced green onions
1/4 cup diced water chestnuts

1/2 cup Miracle Whip
1 tbsp soy sauce
1/8 tsp English mustard powder
salt and ground white pepper
1/2 cup vegetable oil

In a large mixing bowl, place all ingredients except oil. Use your hands to blend mixture thoroughly. Divide the mixture into 16 equal portions and form into patties, approximately 3/4-inch thick. In a 12-inch cast iron skillet, heat oil over medium-high heat. Fry patties until golden brown on each side. Remove and keep warm. Serve cakes with your favorite dipping sauce.

Prep Time: 30 Minutes   **Serves**: 6-8

Square Skillet
From a current Lodge Cast Iron Catalog

Pan-Fried Oregon River Trout

Oregon is a trout fisherman's paradise. Many of the local streams are well kept secrets of the avid fly fisherman in search of Rainbow, Brook and German Browns. Cook the fresh fish within a few hours of catching them!

Ingredients:

6 (5-7 ounce fillets) fresh trout
1 cup flour
1 cup grated or chopped
   hazelnuts (filberts)
salt and fresh white pepper

eggwash (2 eggs and 1/2 cup
   water, blended)
1 cup vegetable oil
lemon slices

NOTE: Filberts or hazelnuts may be grated using a hand grater or chopped fine in a food processor using a metal blade.

In a large mixing bowl place flour, hazelnuts, salt and pepper. Using a fork, blend ingredients thoroughly. In a 14-inch cast iron skillet, heat oil over medium-high heat. Dredge the fish first in the flour mixture, second in the egg wash and then again in the flour mixture. Fry trout until golden brown on both sides, approximately 4 minutes. Remove fish from skillet and keep warm. Garnish with lemon slices.

Prep Time: 20 Minutes   **Serves:** 6

"Once seasoned, always seasoned" is not true.

Beef Short Ribs *with* Ale & Vegetables

Oregon is the micro-brewing capital of the Northwest. Many different lagers, ales and stouts are produced and consumed daily. Each micro-brewery boasts of delicious recipes to accompany its brew.

Ingredients:

6 pounds beef short ribs
2 cups ale
2 cups diced carrots
2 cups diced celery
8 small new potatoes, halved
1/2 cup vegetable oil
8 slices of bacon

2 cups diced onions
2 tbsps brown sugar
1/4 cup Dijon mustard
1/2 tbsp salt
1/2 tbsp black pepper
1/2 tbsp allspice
4 cups beef stock

Preheat oven to 325 degrees F. In a 10-quart cast iron Dutch oven, heat oil over medium-high heat. Add short ribs, three to four at a time, and cook until golden brown. Remove and keep warm. Discard all oil except 1 tablespoon. Add bacon and cook 2-3 minutes to render fat. Return ribs to the pot. Add onions, brown sugar, mustard, salt, pepper, allspice, beef stock and ale. Bring mixture to a rolling boil. Cover and braise in oven for 1 1/2 hours. Remove from oven and add carrots, celery and potatoes. Return pot to the oven and bake until vegetables are tender, approximately 45 minutes. Serve hot with fresh Indian Fry Bread

Prep Time: 2 1/2 Hours   **Serves:** 8

Remove over-seasoning buildup with an abrasive pad, then re-season.

Wild Mushroom Gratin *with* Roasted Filberts

Oregon is one of the richest and most productive mushroom regions in the world. Morel, Chanterelle, Boletus, Matsutake, Lobster, Chicken of the Woods, Yellow Foot, Black Trumpet and Cauliflower are some of the many varieties grown in the Oregon forest. Many varieties are available from April to December each year.

Ingredients:

2 pounds assorted wild
    mushrooms
1 cup roasted hazelnuts
    (filberts), chopped

1/2 cup olive oil
10 ounces Oregon bleu cheese,
    crumbled
salt and fresh black pepper

Preheat oven to 400 degrees F. Clean, trim and slice mushrooms. In a 12-inch cast iron skillet, heat olive oil over medium-high heat. Add mushrooms and saute until most of the juice evaporates. Sprinkle bleu cheese crumbles and hazelnuts over the mushrooms. Season to taste using salt and pepper. Place skillet in oven and bake until cheese melts, approximately 15 minutes. Serve as a side dish with your favorite entree. NOTE: If using dried mushrooms, use only one pound and soak in boiling water for 25 minutes prior to sauteing.

Prep Time: 30 Minutes   **Serves:** 6-8

Top-O-Stove Broiler
From a current Lodge Cast Iron Catalog

Indian Fry Bread

Indian Fry Bread is a part of many Native American Indians' food heritage handed down by generations. It can be eaten with virtually any combination of food that the Northwest has to offer.

Ingredients:

3 cups all purpose flour
3 tsps baking powder

2 cups milk
1/2 cup vegetable oil

In a small mixing bowl, sift dry ingredients together. Make a well in the center and gradually add milk. Using your hands, mix until soft dough forms. Add additional milk to attain proper consistency. Knead the dough until smooth and firm. Cover with plastic wrap and let rest for 10 minutes. Flatten the dough to the thickness of a pizza crust. Cut out 2" x 2" squares. In a 12-inch cast iron skillet, heat oil over medium-high heat. Fry several pieces of dough at a time until golden brown, turning occasionally, approximately 6-7 minutes. Serve with your favorite dish.

Prep Time: 30 Minutes   **Serves:** 6-8

Stove Hollow Ware — Long Pan
From a 1920s Lodge Cast Iron Catalog

Do not store cooked food in cast iron.

Mixed Berry Cobbler

The Pacific Northwest is home to some of the best berries in the world. In most towns and cities, the whole family can pick fresh raspberries, blackberries, marionberries, strawberries and blueberries at local U-Pick farms. After tasting their way through the ripe wonderful berries, many families stock up for the cool winter days.

Ingredients:

1 cup raspberries
1 cup strawberries
2 cups blackberries
1 cup blueberries
3/4 cup sugar

juice of 1 lemon
1 cup flour
3/4 cup sugar
2 cups margarine

Preheat oven to 350 degrees F. In a 12-inch cast iron skillet, place berries. Sprinkle 3/4 cup of sugar and lemon juice over berries. In a small mixing bowl, combine flour, remaining 3/4 cup of sugar and margarine. Place flour mixture over the berries and bake for 30 minutes. Serve with Vanilla Bean Ice Cream. NOTE: Frozen berries may be substituted.

Prep Time: 45 Minutes   **Serves**: 8

Polished Hollow Ware — Straight Kettle, Flat Bottom
From a 1920s Lodge Cast Iron Catalog

Chapter 8
Heartland

America's Heartland or Midwest, with its stockyards and fertile soils, is home to many ingredients we all rely on for our daily menus. It is this north central region of the United States which calls to mind platters of prime ribs, thick and juicy steaks, wheat breads, chicken and dumplings, baked potatoes, and good old fashioned bar-b-que.

Although its boundaries are debated, it is generally considered to be comprised of the 12 states located in the north central U.S. The vast area was first settled by French trappers and explorers who came to the region in the mid 17th century. The wild, untamed wilderness, raging rivers and vast fields of grasses and grains attracted them to stay. The agricultural value of the land soon became apparent.

Some of the early settlers were immigrants who were political and religious refugees, while some were colonists given incentives by the government to move west and others were just seeking their fortunes. The European settlers came in waves beginning in the early 19th century from Sweden, Germany, England and Ireland. With them came such dishes as sauerkraut and dumplings.

Today, the Midwest is identified by its areas known as the Corn belt, Dairy belt and Wheat belt. More than half of the acreage in the Midwest is used to grow wheat, with corn following as another staple crop. Beef is, of course, a major part of the Midwesterners' diet due to the vast open plains and availability of grass and other feeds for cattle and livestock. The Kansas City stockyards top the list of America's largest feeder markets.

The readily-available dairy products are used by innovative chefs to create dishes such as roasted potato dumplings with apples, cream and Amish blue cheese, and cream of garlic soup with a dumpling of spinach, tomato and cheese. The methods of cooking beef vary greatly from roasting to braising, but bar-b-que remains a local, and nationwide, favorite.

Dishes that can be found in America's Heartland include

pork-applesauce-kraut bake, chopped beef pasties, and of course, just about the best steak around. The cultural heritage of the immigrants, the influence of the early Native Americans, and the vast resources of the Heartland region make this cuisine one of America's favorites.

Chef Dennis Bahm

While he spent time at the Culinary Institute of America in Hyde Park, New York, Chef Dennis Bahm has always known that his heart belongs in the Heartland region. It was there that he gained exposure to the traditional cooking of Native Americans and trained to prepare these specialty dishes using indigenous foods.

He has been the executive chef at the Holiday Inn Rushmore Plaza for the last six years. Prior to his move to South Dakota, he spent 18 years in Colorado and Montana as a chef for the John Q. Hammons Company, owner of several hotel chains.

Heartland cuisine was born of two cultures that inhabited this part of the United States more than 100 years ago. Because of long, harsh winters and seasonal hunting, Native Americans were forced to hunt as needed and relied on corn and wheat recipes for sustenance. When the chuckwagon crews began discovering the heartland, they relied on cast iron pots because they were easy to carry and multi-purpose. As a result of the two cultures, the traditional food of the heartland mixes the tortillas and game recipes of the Native Americans with the stews, pot roasts and soups of the pioneers.

With a flare of his own, Chef Bahm prepares traditional heartland dishes—nutritional, energy-producing food that sticks to your ribs. "One-pot stews, chilis and hearty soups are perfectly prepared in cast iron pots. Fajita meats, muffins and steak platters prepared in cast iron stay warm and delicious."

Campfire Fruit Bake

The wild fruits and berries growing across the plains of the Heartland were the main source of desserts to satisfy the early settlers' desires for sweets.

Ingredients:

6 whole apples, peeled
1 tbsp arrowroot
1/2 cup apple cider
2 1/2 cups apple cider

2 tsps ground cinnamon
1/2 cup brown sugar
1/2 cup pure maple syrup
2 cups corn bread mix

Blend arrowroot in 1/2 cup apple cider and set aside. In a 7-quart cast iron dutch oven, place 2 1/2 cups apple cider over medium-high heat. Bring mixture to a rolling boil. Add cinnamon, brown sugar and maple syrup. Using a wire whisk, stir until well blended. Add arrowroot mixture, stirring constantly. Add apples. Return mixture to a rolling boil and reduce heat to simmer. Sprinkle in corn bread mix and blend thoroughly into the apple cider mixture. Cover and allow to cook for 2 hours.

Prep Time: 3 Hours   **Serves:** 6

Cast Iron Loaf Pan
From a current Lodge Cast Iron Catalog

Lodge is the oldest family-owned cookware manufacturer in the country.

Cheese & Corn Bread Lodge-Style

Many colors of corn grew in fields across the country, and it was used for many different things. This combination of vegetables and corn bread is one of my favorites, and the cheese enriches its flavor. I think you will enjoy preparing it.

Ingredients:

12 ears of corn, shuck-on
1/4 cup butter
1 cup diced onion
1 cup diced green bell pepper

1 cup diced red bell pepper
1 cup heavy whipping cream
1 cup grated cheddar cheese
2 cups corn bread mix

Preheat oven to 350 degrees F. Place corn in a cast iron roaster or large dutch oven. Bake for 30 minutes, turning the corn once or twice during the roasting process. Remove from oven and allow to cool. When corn is cool, remove its silk. Using a paring knife, slice the kernels from the cobs. In a 5-quart cast iron Dutch oven, melt butter over medium-high heat. Add onions and peppers. Saute until vegetables are wilted, approximately 3-5 minutes. Add corn and cream. Bring mixture to a rolling boil and reduce to simmer. Add cheese and stir constantly until it is completely melted. Sprinkle in corn bread mix and cover. Bake for 30 minutes or until corn bread is slightly browned and firm to the touch.

Prep Time: 2 Hours **Serves**: 8

Cast iron cookware is formed from 2800 degree molten iron.

Prairie Chicken &
Dumpling Stew

Prairie chicken was abundant in America's Heartland and made a great soup or stew, especially when mixed with fresh spring or winter vegetables. This recipe is particularly good in the fall or winter and can be prepared with game birds as well.

Ingredients:

3 cups chicken meat, diced
1/2 cup butter
2 cups diced onions
2 cups sliced celery
1/2 cup flour
1 quart chicken stock

2 cups sliced carrots
2 cups diced potatoes
2 cups biscuit mix
1 tsp salt
1 tsp black pepper

NOTE: Prepare 2 cups of biscuit mix such as Bisquick, according to package directions. Once biscuit dough is formed, place in a bowl, cover with clear wrap and set aside. In a 7-quart cast iron Dutch oven, melt butter over medium-high heat. Add chicken and saute 5-10 minutes until cooked and lightly browned. Add onions and celery. Saute until vegetables are wilted, approximately 3-5 minutes. Sprinkle in flour, and blend well into the vegetable mixture. Add chicken stock, one ladle at a time, until all is incorporated. Bring mixture to a rolling boil and reduce heat to simmer. Add carrots and potatoes. Continue to cook 10-15 minutes. Season mixture to taste using salt and pepper. Spoon the biscuit mix into the pot in the shape of dumplings. Cover and cook approximately 1 hour. Serve in a soup bowl with a generous amount of the vegetables and a couple of the dumplings.

Prep Time: 1 1/2 Hours   **Serves:** 8

 Remove over-seasoning buildup with an abrasive pad, then re-season.

Beef Potato Bake

Ground buffalo was traditionally used in this recipe, but ground beef works just as well to make a hearty meal on those cold prairie nights. Potatoes were always plentiful in the root cellars across the plains and are a staple in many recipes from the area.

Ingredients:

2 pounds lean ground beef
4 large potatoes, cut into
    1/2-inch cubes
1 cup diced onions
1/2 cup diced celery
2 tbsps chopped garlic
2 tbsps sage
1 egg

2 tbsps salt
1 tbsp cracked black pepper
1/2 cup Italian bread crumbs
1 cup flour
1 cup grape jelly
3 cups ketchup
1/2 cup water

Preheat oven to 350 degrees F. In a large mixing bowl, combine ground beef , onions, celery, garlic, sage, egg, salt, pepper and bread crumbs. Blend until seasonings are thoroughly incorporated. Form into 2-inch meatballs and coat each lightly in flour. Place the meatballs in a 12-inch cast iron skillet. Bake 20-25 minutes or until meatballs are partially cooked. While meatballs are cooking, combine jelly, ketchup and water in a small mixing bowl. Set aside. When meatballs are cooked, pour off excess fat and top the meatballs with the ketchup mixture. Place potatoes in skillet around the meatballs, cover and bake 45 minutes or until potatoes are tender. **Prep Time:** 1 1/2 Hours **Serves:** 8

2 Cup Melting Pot
From a current Lodge Cast Iron Catalog

Soda Bread, Skillet-Style

This recipe is all about hearth cooking! The thick cast iron skillet gives this recipe its wide open hearth flavor.

Ingredients:

2 cups flour
2 tsps baking soda
2 tsps baking powder
3 tbsps sugar
3 tbsps butter
1 cup buttermilk

1/2 cup raisins
2 tbsps caraway seeds
1/4 cup flour
1 tbsp corn meal
1 tsp coarse salt

Preheat oven to 350 degrees F. In a large mixing bowl, combine 2 cups flour, baking soda, baking powder and sugar. Using a pastry blender, mix all ingredients until thoroughly blended. Cut butter into the flour until mixture reaches the consistency of corn meal. Add buttermilk and continue to blend until moist dough is formed. Fold in the raisins and caraway seeds. Place dough on the floured work surface and knead for 5 minutes. Roll dough out to approximately 1/4-inch thick. Cut the dough into circles the size of a 10-inch cast iron skillet. Place circles of dough into the skillet and cut into 4 pieces, pizza-style. Sprinkle lightly with salt and bake until golden brown, approximately 10-15 minutes. Serve as an accompaniment to salads or main courses.

Prep Time: 2 Hours   **Serves**: 6

Stove Hollow Ware — Round Griddle with Bails
From a 1920s Lodge Cast Iron Catalog

 Cast iron cookware is made from recycled metal.

A Page *from* Our Past . . .

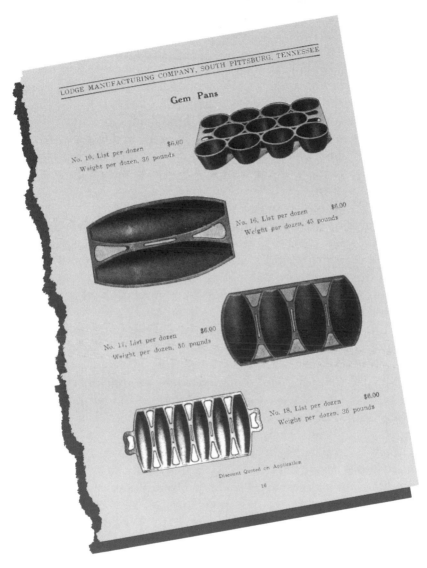

LODGE MANUFACTURING COMPANY, SOUTH PITTSBURG, TENNESSEE

Gem Pans

No. 16, List per dozen $6.00
Weight per dozen, 36 pounds

No. 16, List per dozen $6.00
Weight per dozen, 45 pounds

No. 17, List per dozen $6.00
Weight per dozen, 36 pounds

No. 18, List per dozen $6.00
Weight per dozen, 36 pounds

Discount Quoted on Application

16

From a 1920s Lodge Cast Iron Catalog

Chapter 9
Great Lakes

As you venture to the Great Lakes region of the United States, you will find a rich history and foods indicative of the lands — its vast waters and flat, fertile plains.

The states of Indiana, Illinois, Michigan, Ohio and Wisconsin comprise the Great Lakes region located in the north-central part of the U.S. Separated from the west by the Mississippi River and from the south by the Ohio River, the region borders Canada to its north.

Although early Indian tribes occupied the lands and waters, closely guarding them from intruders, French explorers Jolliet, Marquette and LaSalle first explored the Great Lakes region in the 1600s. It remained a French territory until 1763 when France granted the region to Britain. From 1803 to 1848, the Great Lakes states entered the Union and settlers were attracted to this bountiful land.

It is not only Americans who settled this sought-after land, but the Dutch, Germans, Scandinavians, Swiss and Cornish immigrants also came together to create this unique culture and cuisine. They brought with them talents for fishing, hunting and farming and a knowledge of growing vegetables and raising dairy cattle. With the Dutch came smoked and salted fish, smoked eel, roasted goose, hearty soups, and rye and whole-grain breads. The Germans contributed their stews, breaded veal, gravy-rich pot roast, wursts, coffee cakes, and cheeses. The ingredients of the Scandinavians included dried beans, cabbage, potatoes and cheeses. And, with the Cornish settlers came Cornish pasty (an individual meat-and-vegetable pie sealed in a pastry crust), scones, English toffee pie and Devonshire cream.

Evidence of these early settlers can be seen in the signature foods of the larger cities of St. Louis, Chicago, Cincinnati and Milwaukee. An example is the German and Scandinavian influence in the cheese-making techniques so popular in Milwaukee.

With its fertile soils and flat plains ideal for farming, the

Great Lakes region produces abundant crops of corn, soybean, wheat and oats, as well as fruit orchards which yield apples, peaches, persimmons, cranberries and cherries. These lands are also suitable for raising cattle, hogs and poultry.

Because of its vast lakes and rivers, the Great Lakes region is probably best known for its plentiful supply of fish. Lake herring, black bass, rainbow trout and salmon are but a few of the popular species which eventually make their way into delicious recipes. The dense woodlands surrounding the lakes are an excellent source of wild game and fowl.

Dishes which typify the Great Lakes region include Pheasant and Wild Rice, Home-Style Fish Boil, Welsh Rabbit, Cornish Pastry, Baked Swiss Cheese Fondue, Green Pea Soup, Braised Celery, Persimmon, Pudding, Cherry Cobbler, Black Walnut Fudge and Cheesecake.

Chef Louis Jesowshek

Chef Louis Jesowshek has been a member of the American Culinary Federation (ACF) since 1972. He is an ACF Certified Executive Chef and a member of the group's prestigious American Academy of Chefs.

He has served as executive chef for the Hilton Hotel Corporation in New Orleans, Dallas and Mobile. He has also served as Chef de Cuisine of the New Orleans Fairmont Hotel's renowned Sazerac Restaurant.

An experienced culinary competitor, Chef Jesowshek now serves as judge and advisor to the most formidable Louisiana culinary shows. In addition he has compiled "An Anthology of Louisiana Cuisine" and recently filmed a PBS special entitled "Lunch Louisiana-Style."

Although Chef Jesowshek is currently the executive chef at Louisiana's largest medical complex, Our Lady of the Lakes Regional Medical Center in Baton Rouge, his roots are deep in the Great Lakes region. In 1992, Chef Jesowshek was named the United States Regional Chef of the Year for the Midwest region, and in 1993, he was a nominee for the Chef's Professionalism Award and the Mid-West Region's nominee for the United States Chef's Professionalism Award.

As a native of the area, he has a special appreciation of the recipes and cooking methods that came to the United States when Germans immigrated to the area in the mid-1800s. He believes that much of the cast iron cookware used by those in the area is still being used by their families today.

"Bratwurst, Rouladen and Kraut dishes are best prepared in cast iron cookware. Because it holds heat and conducts heat faster that any cookware on the market, it is the best thing for frying. Recipes prepared in a Dutch oven have an intensified flavor because the flavor is not lost in the steam—it is infused into the meats and vegetables."

Cast iron is porous and will drink up oil upon seasoning.

Sheboygan Bratwurst

Sheboygan, Wisconsin, is nestled at the foot of Lake Winnebago among the beautiful Kettle Morraine scenery. In the town renowned for its sausages, spicy bratwurst is king. In fact, there is an entire weekend devoted to celebrating this sausage called The Sheboygan Bratwurst Festival. A cold beer always accompanies a "brat."

Ingredients:

6 (4-ounce) bratwurst links
8 ounces beer
1/4 cup butter
1 large onion, sliced

1 red bell pepper, sliced
1 green bell pepper, sliced
1 clove garlic, minced
3 ounces stone ground mustard

Place the bratwurst links into a 12-inch cast iron skillet over medium heat. Add beer and slowly cook the bratwurst until all of the beer evaporates. Remove the bratwurst and keep warm. In the same skillet, melt butter over medium-high heat. Add onions and cook until translucent. Add bell peppers and garlic and continue to cook until tender, approximately 10 minutes. Slice the bratwurst 1/2-inch thick and place in the center of a 10-inch plate. Surround the bratwurst with vegetable mixture and stone ground mustard on the side. This dish may also be served as a hearty sandwich using a potato bun or a sub-loaf.

Prep Time: 30 Minutes   **Serves**:   6

Andirons — Cast Iron
From a 1920s Lodge Cast Iron Catalog

Preheat cast iron before baking.

Great Lakes Potato Soup

Potatoes were the staple of early Midwestern cookery and were usually made into cream-style soups. I find this old variation refreshingly different.

Ingredients:

1 pound red new potatoes
6 cups chicken broth
1 carrot peeled and sliced
   1/8-inch thick
1 leek, sliced white only
1/8 tsp salt

1/8 tsp black pepper
1/4 tsp prepared horseradish
2 slices cooked bacon, crumbled
1/2 tsp chopped parsley
6 slices garlic toast

Leave the potatoes unpeeled as this will add not only nutrients to this dish but also color and flavor. In addition, the skins help the potatoes retain shape during cooking. Slice the potatoes 1/4-inch thick. Pour chicken broth into a 3-quart cast iron dutch oven. Add carrots and leeks and cook for 5 minutes or until vegetables are al dente. Add potatoes and cook until tender, approximately 10-12 minutes. Season to taste using salt and black pepper. Add horseradish and bacon. To serve, place soup in a large soup bowl and garnish with parsley. Serve with garlic toast.

Prep Time: 30 Minutes   **Serves:** 6

Lodge manufactures over 140 items of cast iron cookware.

Friday Fish Fry

On a Friday night in Milwaukee, the question is not what to eat but where to eat. Everyone knows that "Fish Fry" is on the menu. Restaurants, church basements and local taverns all serve their own variation of this local legend. Fish fry is usually served with potato pancakes and homemade tartar sauce.

Ingredients:

4 pounds lake perch fillets
1 tbsp salt
1 tbsp ground white pepper
1 cup flour
1 egg, beaten

1 cup milk
1/8 tsp hot sauce
1/8 tsp Worcestershire sauce
2 cups seasoned bread crumbs
4 cups peanut oil

In a 5-quart cast iron Dutch oven, heat oil to 350 degrees F. Pat fillets dry to remove excess moisture. Season well with salt and pepper. Coat each fillet with flour and set aside. In a separate mixing bowl, combine egg and milk. Season to taste using hot sauce and Worcestershire sauce. Dip floured fillet into egg mixture, drain off excess batter then dredge into seasoned bread crumbs. Place breaded fillets, one at a time, into hot oil. Be careful not to overload the pot so the oil will not maintain its temperature. Cook until the fish are golden brown on each side. Remove and drain on paper towels.

Prep Time: 30 Minutes   **Serves**: 6

Polished Hollow Ware — Bowls, Scotch & Yankee
From a 1920s Lodge Cast Iron Catalog

Sauerbraten

In the days before refrigeration, there were many ways to preserve meats. One of the best was pickling, It was acceptable to hold the beef in a brine for up to a week. Customarily, four days were considered optimum. This hearty dish can only be cooked properly in a Dutch oven.

Ingredients:

5 pound beef chuck roast
2 cups cider vinegar
2 cups water
1 large onion, sliced
1 carrot, sliced
1 rib of celery, sliced
1 bay leaf
1 tsp peppercorns
1/4 cup sugar

1 tsp black pepper
1 tsp garlic, minced
1/4 cup vegetable oil
1 tsp salt
1/4 cup brown sugar
2 tbsps vegetable oil
2 tbsps flour
1/4 cup raisins

Preheat oven to 325 degrees F. Place cider vinegar, water, onions, carrots and celery into a 5-quart cast iron Dutch oven over medium-high heat. Bring mixture to a rolling boil. Add bay leaf, peppercorns and sugar. Remove from heat and keep warm. Place chuck roast in a large bowl. Rub roast completely with pepper and garlic. Pour warm cider vinegar mixture over the roast to marinate. Cover bowl with clear wrap and refrigerate for 24 hours, turning occasionally. The longer you marinate, the more sour the roast will taste. Remove the roast from the marinade and reserve the liquid for later use. Using the same Dutch oven, heat 1/4 cup vegetable oil over medium-high heat. Add roast and sear on all sides until completely browned. Pour the reserved marinade, salt and brown sugar over the roast and cover. Place in oven and cook for 3-4 hours, until tender. Remove roast from Dutch oven and keep warm. Strain cooking juices and set aside. In a 10-inch cast iron skillet, combine 2 tablespoons each of vegetable oil and flour. Using a wire whisk, stir constantly until a dark brown roux is achieved. Add reserved cooking liquids and blend to a sauce-like consistency. Bring mixture to a rolling boil, reduce heat to simmer and cook 5 minutes. Slice roast and serve with gravy. Garnish with raisins. **Prep Time:** 4 Hours **Serves:** 6

Rhubarb Dampfnudlen

Spring brings forth magnificent rhubarb. So energetic is this harbinger of Spring that its stalks often break through the crust of residual snow impatiently awaiting its first taste of Spring. This hearty vegetable is usually treated like a fruit and baked into pies and cobblers. However, beware of the leaves as they are poisonous. Here is an old-fashioned recipe I remember from my childhood days on a dairy farm. I have never seen it prepared in anything except cast iron.

Ingredients:

1 pound rhubarb,
   cut 1-inch long
1/2 tbsp active dry yeast
1 tbsp sugar
1 1/4 cups all purpose flour
1/2 cup warm milk
   (100 degrees F)

1/2 cup strawberry jam
1/2 cup sugar
1/8 tsp nutmeg
1 tbsp butter
2 tbsps sugar
1/2 tsp salt
1 egg

Preheat oven to 350 degrees F. In a large mixing bowl, combine yeast, 1 tablespoon of sugar and 1 1/4 cups flour. Add warm milk to flour mixture and blend well to form dough. The warm milk will activate the yeast, causing the dough to rise. Cover the mixture with a dry cloth and place in a warm area to rise for approximately 1 hour. While the dough is rising, coat an 8-inch cast iron skillet with the strawberry jam. Layer the rhubarb pieces on top of the jam until all are used. Sprinkle rhubarb with sugar and nutmeg. Cover and bake for 15 minutes. Remove and allow to cool slightly. In a large bowl, cream butter, 2 tablespoons of sugar and salt. Add egg and continue to whip until light and fluffy. Fold egg mixture into the rhubarb, blending thoroughly. Using an ice cream scoop, place the dough, in dumpling fashion, over the rhubarb. Cover the skillet and return rhubarb to oven. Bake until rhubarb is thoroughly cooked, approximately 45 minutes-1 hour. Remove and serve warm with vanilla ice cream.

Prep Time: 2 1/2 Hours   **Serves:** 6

Boiling hot water and a brush are all you need for washing and cleaning cast iron.

Skillet Raisin Bread

Ingredients:

1 cup raisins
2 cups all purpose flour
1 1/2 tsps double-acting baking
   powder
1/2 tsp baking soda
1/2 tsp salt

1 tbsp sugar
1/4 cup shortening, chilled
1 tsp cinnamon powder
1 egg, beaten
2/3 cup buttermilk
1 ounce milk

Preheat oven to 375 degrees F. Grease a 4" x 8" cast iron loaf pan. In a large mixing bowl, sift together flour, baking powder, baking soda, salt and sugar. Using a pastry blender, cut shortening into the flour mixture until it reaches the consistency of coarse corn meal. Stir in raisins and cinnamon. In a separate mixing bowl, combine egg and buttermilk. Add flour mixture and blend well until all is incorporated. Pour batter into skillet until evenly distributed. Brush the dough with 1 ounce of milk. Cover and bake for 35-40 minutes.

Prep Time: 1 1/2 Hours   **Serves:** 6

Perch Pan
From a current Lodge Cast Iron Catalog

 If the pan is well seasoned, nothing will stick to cast iron.

Bavarian Red Cabbage

The Heartland has very cold winters. Traditionally, winter vegetables were in abundance. The Midwestern root cellar was the pantry of the past. Here, the potatoes, carrots and cabbages kept well into the spring. The red cabbage brought vivid color to the usually drab winter table. This is one of my grandmother's favorite recipes, and I hope you will enjoy it as I do. She served it with game and leftovers. It was often served cold the next day as a wonderful, colorful salad.

Ingredients:

2 pounds red cabbage
1 cinnamon stick
1 ounce red wine vinegar
1/4 tsp black pepper
1/8 tsp salt

4 slices bacon, cut 1-inch thick
1/2 large onion, diced
1/2 cup applesauce
1/4 cup red wine vinegar
2 tbsps sugar

Remove the outer leaves of the cabbage, core and shred. In a large mixing bowl, place cabbage, cinnamon, 1 ounce red wine vinegar, black pepper and salt. Refrigerate overnight. In a 5-quart cast iron Dutch oven, saute bacon until golden brown and crisp. Add onions and saute until wilted, approximately 3-5 minutes. Remove cabbage from marinade and discard marinade. Place cabbage in onion mixture, stirring well. Add applesauce, 1/4 cup red wine vinegar and sugar. Cover Dutch oven, reduce heat to simmer and cook approximately 1 hour. NOTE: Do not overcook, as cabbage will lose color.

Prep Time: 1 Hour 15 Minutes   **Serves:** 6

Cast iron is one of the "Top Ten" essentials for any kitchen.

Index